THE POWER OF ONE

Christian Living in the Third Millennium

THE POWER OF ONE

Christian Living in the Third Millennium

Msgr. Jim Lisante

Resurrection Press
An Imprint of
CATHOLIC BOOK PUBLISHING CO.
Totowa • New Jersey

Dedication

This book is dedicated to Frank and Lena Lisante, and Louise and James McNeal. These were my grandparents, and the people who planted the seeds that blossomed into my life. I am forever grateful for their many sacrifices.

Grateful acknowledgement is made to *The Christophers* to reproduce essays contained in these pages.

First published in March 2004 by
Catholic Book Publishing/Resurrection Press
77 West End Road
Totowa, NJ 07512

Copyright © 2004 by The Christophers

ISBN 1-878718-84-3
Library of Congress Catalog Card Number: 2002116875

All rights reserved. No part of this book may be reproduced or transmitted in any form or by any means, electronic or mechanical, including photocopying, recording, or by any information storage and retrieval system without permission in writing from the publisher.

Cover design by John Murello
Cover photo by Danny Feld
Printed in the United States of America

Contents

Acknowledgments

SPECIAL thanks to all who work or have worked at The Christophers. Wonderful, dedicated and generous souls who live the motto "Better to light one candle than to curse the darkness."

In particular, I thank Dennis Heaney, President of the Christophers, and Gerald Costello and Stephanie Raha for many years of editing the columns in this volume.

My personal assistant Elaine Harman deserves continued thanks for her valiant attempts to coordinate my ministry. And my gratitude is warmly offered to Emilie Cerar of Resurrection Press and Catholic Book Publishing for her wonderful work in seeing this book through to publication.

Last but never least, thanks to Cecelia, Nicholas, Joan, Patti, Jim, Bob, Jonathan, Matthew, Anthony, Marisa, and Julia for being the family I love always.

Foreword

BRUCE Campbell is a popular actor of both movies and television. His film "Army of Darkness" is one of the most well known cult movies in America. Bruce wrote a book called *If Chins Could Kill*. It's the tale of trying to make it in Hollywood. Bruce Campbell and I had a similar experience. We've been interviewed by the author of this book, Msgr. Jim Lisante. Listen to what Bruce says in his book about that experience:

"Media, in all its hydra forms, is a creature unto itself. I got a first-hand experience in New York City, on a single day, of just how different markets and sensibilities can be.

"Around midday, I had a TV interview with Msgr. Jim Lisante, a priest who had his own television show in Manhattan. Monsignor Jim and I talked, uninterrupted, for a half hour and we got into some real life issues: life, death, morality—you name it. The experience was fairly intense, but very fulfilling.

"As a host, Monsignor Jim had clearly read my book and took great pains to point out very obscure facts. His questions were both insightful and unique, and by the end of my visit we parted feeling like old pals.

" 'Wow. Okay, so that was pretty amazing. Where to next?' I asked my publicity boss."

Yes, Monsignor Jim Lisante is pretty amazing. In his insight. In his work as one of the best Catholic media people we've got. And in his writing ability.

I so admire Monsignor Jim Lisante. He's such a normal guy, a profound thinker, a devoted priest. And he realizes the need for effective communication. I'm so glad he has written *The Power of One* because people need to read more and more these days about their faith and the Catholic Church.

Contrary to current popular perceptions, Monsignor Jim is what typifies a Catholic priest. He is intelligent, prayerful, devoted, humble, modestly paid and hard working. His words and the delightful, upbeat, enthusiastic manner in which he expresses them, make this book a great read.

I recommend *The Power of One* with great enthusiasm. It celebrates everything we need to believe. The vital importance of the individual. The absolute gift of human life. The value of each of us, individually created by God who has a unique plan for every human person.

The Christopher message needs to be heard, now more than ever. Monsignor Jim Lisante is a wonderful spokesperson for this vital message. Please read it with great joy like I did!

Catherine Hicks
Star of "7th Heaven"

Introduction

IN 1945, following a war like no other, Father James Keller founded a movement called the Christophers. It had a basic and simple philosophy. It claimed that "You can make a difference." It told each of us that "there's no one else like you." Out of this came a movement that used the popular media to inspire countless millions. Father Keller, a Maryknoll Missioner, believed in the value of every human person. In this he was prophetic.

He prophesized the Second Vatican Council in its emphasis on the huge impact Christian laypeople can have on our needful world. Father Keller also anticipated the universal struggle that would so occupy our public discourse in the great debate on the inherent value of human life. If you believe that every life matters, that every life is the product of God's plan, then you've got to be a defender of the human person, born or preborn.

It's my privilege to carry on the message of Father James Keller. I've been the author of his column, "Light One Candle," for several years. They are, happily, published in over three hundred and fifty newspapers. Many of the recent columns are contained in this volume. May they serve to remind us of the precious value of every human life. May they help us to know that no person is a mistake or an accident. Rather, we are meant to be here. We are, all of us, children of a God who wants us to do what no one else can do the way that we'll do it. May we, each of us, own this noble calling and live it fully.

In the Lord of Love and Life,

James D. Lisante

Part I
Random Acts of
Kindness

Thank You for Asking

IN the twenty years I've been a priest, I've spent a lot of time sitting and listening to people. In fact, listening is probably the activity ministers of all faiths do most. Now, some people would balk at the notion of listening as an activity. After all, it sounds pretty passive. You're not physically exerting yourself. It's not manual labor. But it is, nonetheless, a real activity. True listening involves an active disposition, it requires a lively intellect and must always be accompanied by the ability to hear beyond the "audio," taking in the fuller meaning of both the words spoken and the words that aren't.

One expert suggested that pastoral counseling (that's what they call what we do), involves listening with a combination of heart, mind and soul: the heart to have true compassion or empathy for the person sitting before you, the mind to know how to direct the person to a safer harbor, and the soul to acknowledge that God works through everyone, even those most resistant to His plan.

There are two approaches counselors use. The image of the more passive counselor is the popular notion from television and the movies of someone taking notes either on paper or mentally, but saying very little. This is the quiet listener who hopes that just giving the person a chance to speak will lead to a solution. And, in fact, sometimes that does happen. People who are bottled up are often helped just by having the chance to articulate their struggles and choices. Others require more active or direct counseling. They need to be helped to focus and decide on a course of action or behavior. As a pastoral counselor, I probably fall into this category. I think that people are looking for us to tell them what we think. They may not agree with us. They may not think much of the advice, but many do want a reaction. They want to know what we make of the story they've just shared.

People who come to counseling are generally honing in on a problem they face. And that sometimes finds them pretty self-absorbed. Understandably, folks come because of personal pain, stress or confusion. Once in a while, though, something interesting happens—just as it did very recently, during the visit of a man I'll call Steven. Steven came to me with a host of family and personal problems. Frankly, they were heartbreaking to hear. It's going to take a lot of time for him to resolve his many crises. But then, in the midst of his sad story, Steven did something that others rarely do. He stopped talking about himself and his problems. He looked at me directly and asked: "Sorry for all this talk about me and my problems. I know you've had a rough year, what with the loss of your closest friend to cancer. Father Jim, how are you doing?"

I think I was more taken aback by the fact that he cared than by the particular question. I gave a fairly ordinary answer, then added with great sincerity, "but thank you, Steve, for bothering to ask."

Everyone wants to be heard. Listening is a gift we share with others. Listening well is a grace for people in pain. Knowing that someone cares can be communicated in many ways: through touch, through physical assistance and, most importantly, by the quality of our ability to hear with compassion. Sometimes we take these goodhearted listeners for granted. Since they've always "lent us an ear" we presume they always will. And maybe that's so. But as a professional in the listening business I need to tell you —it's great to be heard too. It's wonderful to have someone who stops long enough to ask: "How are you doing?"

Take the time to speak honestly. But remember to take your turn and listen, too.

Question for Reflection

● Think of a time when you listened with your "third ear" and how you responded. Now remember a time when someone "heard" you. How did it make you feel?

The Reason for the Season

EACH year, on Christmas Eve, our parish has a Mass for children and their parents, which is beyond jammed! Our Church seats about nine hundred people, but on this night, no fewer than fifteen hundred folks show up. Happily, we have a lower church that can handle the spillover. This Mass has an absolute flavor of joy. The music soars, and everyone sings out in a way they rarely do during the rest of the year. Little children's anticipation of the birthday of Jesus adds a crackle of energy.

At the end of the priest's homily, a special visitor is introduced—it's Santa Claus himself. Santa engages in a brief dialogue with the priest celebrant. Santa reminds everyone that the reason for the season is Christ, that it's far better to give than to receive and that communal prayer is important. He then stays for the rest of the Mass. The wonder in the eyes of the children (and their parents) is thrilling to see.

A few years ago, the Muller family attended this very special Christmas Eve Mass. They felt the contagious joy and thought it should be shared even more widely. So they stopped me outside church and asked, "How many people in the parish can't get to Christmas Mass because they're homebound, disabled or unable to get out and about?" My guess at that time was that at least a hundred people were unable to come to church, most of them elderly parishioners fighting illness or disability. Richard, the father of that family, said that he thought missing such a wonderful Christmas celebration was a sad thing. I agreed, but what could be done?

Richard and Mary Muller went home and found a way. They own a thriving photography and videography studio. Their job is saving and sharing joyous moments in people's lives. So they made a proposal and then made good on it by donating their work. On Christmas Eve, they would bring their camera crew, including their two teenage sons, Gregory and Keith, and film that joyous and uplifting Mass with Santa and the children. They'd then return to the studio, edit what they'd shot and reproduce a hundred videocassettes. Our job was relatively simple: to see that each of the homebound parishioners got a copy and had a VCR to watch it. Our Eucharistic Ministers gladly acted as delivery agents.

The reaction from the senior citizens and homebound was immediate and uniformly positive.

One letter I received, from a ninety-year-old woman, sixty-seven years in the parish community, said it best: "Being alone at Christmas isn't easy. But with the special gift of the Christmas Eve video, I wasn't alone any more. Christmas is always better when seen through the eyes of children. I became one with the young people of St. Thomas thanks to the miracle of that tape. Thanks so much for letting me be a part of that joy-filled evening of celebration. Maybe I can't walk or get out, but through the efforts of our parish, I wasn't cut off from the party!"

This "Christopher moment" happened because one person in one company decided to make a difference for others by combining business know-how and heart-felt good will. If every individual and every business worked this way, what a huge gift of hope and joy we could bring to our waiting world.

Question for Reflection

● Share an experience of a joint effort to love your neighbor. How was it received?

At Work for the Master Builder

"**H**ow ya doin? How's the job?"

For a growing group of people today the answer is: "I've been laid off." The numbers are not huge yet, and, hopefully, the economy will soon turn around. But that still leaves thousands of people who, a year ago, thought they had steady jobs in growing industries now searching for work to support themselves and their families.

Anyone of a certain age knows we've been down this road before, yet it's still a shock when signing bonuses give way to pink slips. More than that, many people's identities are so tightly bound to what they do for a living that, for better or worse, they see themselves in terms of their job titles, perhaps more than any other aspect of their lives. Let me say flat out that as a priest I really do not know what it's like to be out of work and, considering the vocation shortage, I am never likely to experience it. So if you're thinking, "Easy for you to say!" I can't argue. Still, I have seen again and again through members of my parish the painful sense of loss as well as the host of financial problems that unemployment causes.

In September 2001, the U.S. Catholic Bishops issued a Labor Day statement offering a reminder about the dignity of people who are far more important than things, including jobs. The document goes on to say, "In Genesis, we come to understand that human beings, created in God's image, share in the tasks of the Creator through their work. . . . Work is for the person, not the person for work."

The fact is each and every person has an individual God-given mission in life. This mission certainly includes work, but it goes well beyond that. Whether you are pulling down a six-figure salary or reading the want ads, the task of changing the world for the better in some unique way is still yours and yours alone. You will never fulfill your role in the workplace alone, but in your home and your community as well. Easy for me to say? Yes. It also happens to be the truth.

Over twenty years ago in El Salvador, Archbishop Oscar Romero was martyred because he stood up for the economic and political rights of his people. A man who took his own mission and that of others very seriously, he had this to say about the real meaning of work: "It helps, now and then, to step back and take the long view. The Kingdom is not only beyond our efforts; it is beyond our vision. We accomplish in our lifetime only a tiny fraction of the magnificent enterprise that is the Lord's work. . . .

"We cannot do everything and there is a sense of liberation in realizing that. This enables us to do something, and to do it very, very well. It may be incomplete, but it is a beginning, a step along the way, an opportunity for the Lord's grace to enter and do the rest.

"We may never see the end results, but that is the difference between the Master Builder and the worker. We are workers, but not master builders . . . ministers, not messiahs.

"We are prophets of a future that is not our own."

Whatever challenges we face—sickness, family strife, financial setbacks—God still asks us to serve His people, even if we can't always understand the how and why of it all. We are the Master Builder's workers.

Question for Reflection

● Reflect on the inspiring words of Archbishop Oscar Romero on the real meaning of work. As one of the Master Builder's workers, write a letter to God describing your response to Him.

All about Giving

THE good news is we're giving more to charity than ever before. According to recent studies of American generosity, in the year 2000 we donated a little over *$203 billion* to charitable causes. The further positive news is that this amount represents an increase of 3.2% over the previous year. Putting it in even more striking comparative terms, in 1990 our collective giving amounted to slightly more than $100 billion a year. So comparing current figures to those from a decade ago should give us a reason to rejoice. It would seem that we have learned the biblical injunction about the joy and value of giving.

But as with much in life, figures can be deceiving. The numbers show that *2001* represents the smallest increase in giving over the past five years. Total donations to the needy represent less than 2% of our gross national product. In other words, we do give, but we have a lot more we could be giving.

There are many theories about why we give at the relatively small levels we do. Some suggest it's because we expect the government to take care of problems, believing that our taxes can handle the needs of those in society who fall between the cracks. Yet, cutbacks in government-supported social programs have left millions of people in need of alternative support systems. While government certainly plays an important role, looking after others can never be its exclusive concern. For the needy to be truly covered requires the voluntary involvement of the larger society, in other words, you and me.

Other experts say we give with a skewered view of the real price of helping. We may think that the five or ten dollar check we send to a favorite charitable organization is enough. But think about it. What does five or ten dollars buy in today's market? Not very much. A recent monthly electrical bill for the parish where I am pastor came to $8,000. It takes a lot of fives and tens just to keep the lights on.

So how should we determine what's a fair measure for giving? Maybe we have only to examine our spending. When I look at my charge card bills, I see money spent on books (one volume was $25), two compact disks at $16 each, and $8 tickets to the movies for a friend and me. During one billing period, I spent $73 for my entertainment.

In the same period, I mailed checks to some very worthy charities for about $30.

Does that mean that my giving lacks value? Of course not! But, if I can spend $73 on my transitory enjoyment, aren't the needs of poor, sick and needy people worthy of a comparable generosity? There's nothing wrong with buying things that we enjoy. But if our spending were matched by donations to charities that depend on us, our neighbors and our consciences would be better served.

At the end of last year, I sat down and examined my budget. In the final breakdown, it came down to this: over 80% of my spending was for my own needs or pleasures; about 15% was spent on others in my family for birthday and Christmas gifts, dinners, etc. That left about 5% of my money to be spent on the poor, the dispossessed, the broken and the sick in body, mind or spirit.

I know that 5% isn't bad, but I also know that "I am my brother's keeper" and my sister's, too. Not only can I do more, I must.

Question for Reflection

● Do you agree with Father Jim that giving 5% of your money to the poor and sick is not enough? What will help you to up the ante?

Evaluating Ourselves

THE seminary is a mystery to most people. They know it's a place people go to prepare themselves for ministry, but what happens there is often unknown. It's really not complicated. To work in religious life you need knowledge; you study theology and philosophy. It's also a place of prayer, since developing a personal relationship with God is essential. Whether or not someone is destined to be ordained is left to a group of advisors, or evaluators. Let me share with you one rather unusual story of evaluation.

During my time in the seminary, a written synopsis of faculty opinion would be given to each student on one's readiness for promotion. Needless to say, the evaluation sheet was a source of high anxiety. One of the best and brightest students, diligent in his work, faithful to his prayer life and just an all-around great candidate for priesthood was my friend Joe. But, like all of us, Joe didn't always believe that his goodness was so apparent. He worried that he might not be voted on to the next level of preparation for ordination.

Another classmate, Tony, picked up on Joe's insecurities. Finding a blank form discarded by a faculty member, Tony proceeded to author a bogus evaluation of Joe. Forms were usually dropped off at our rooms at dinner time. I happened to be with Joe when he saw the form envelope tucked under his door. He went to his room to study the assessment of his priestly candidacy. About fifteen minutes later, he was in my room, looking like he'd lost everything. "Well," said Joe, "I guess it's all over for me. They want me gone." The evaluation would certainly lead anyone to the same conclusion. It criticized Joe about everything: his studies, his personality, his multiple inabilities. In short, it was a devastating indictment of this good man.

Knowing Joe well, I responded: "Hey, they got it all wrong. This doesn't describe you at all. You've got to challenge this,

Joe." But Joe would have none of it. If the faculty thought so lit-tle of him, then maybe it was time for him to go. In his face I saw all his hopes vanished. It was a sorry sight.

Not five minutes later, Tony entered the room, picked the evaluation out of Joe's still trembling hands and ripped it into little pieces. Joe shouted "what are you doing?" Tony, laughing and still not realizing the impact his trick had made, told him lightly, "It's not a real evaluation, dopey. I wrote it myself. Just wanted to see you react!" Joe was relieved that he wouldn't be booted from the seminary, but ticked off at the cruelty of the joke.

I think most of us react more like Joe than we should. Joe was none of the negative things described in that report. He was just the opposite. Goodhearted and kind, prayerful and generous, hardworking and intelligent, Joe was a great candi-date for ministry. But like most of us, he relied on others in for-mulating his self-vision. If people said he was bad or weak or lacking character, he believed it! After all, someone else said it. It's got to be true, right? No. Our inner compass, our sense of ourselves, our understanding of our inherent worth and value, shouldn't be dependent on the whimsical feelings others have about us. We are valuable because we're made by the Creator, because we share a mutual human dignity. Every single one of us matters very much. And no arbitrary evaluation or judg-ment should be the determining factor in our own self view.

I wish my friend, on reading that evaluation, had been able to look in the mirror and say "they got it wrong. They don't really know me. I'll have to let them in on who I truly am." Instead he believed what he'd been told by others. The inner voice of our personal truth should be the final determination of our value, a voice filtered through the prism of our inestimable value as children of a God who does not make mistakes.

Questions for Reflection

- Remember a time when your self esteem was negatively influenced by the criticism of another. What defense can you employ on your behalf in the future?

- How have you helped another person understand their inherent goodness?

Build Up, Don't Tear Down

NOT too long ago two ancient statues known as the Great Buddhas of Bamiyan in Afghanistan were destroyed. These imposing figures, over a hundred feet tall and hewn from the rock of a mountain 1500 years ago, were not ruined by natural disaster, but rather by deliberate demolition.

The area was controlled by the fundamentalist Taliban which believes that idols are forbidden by their faith. An outcry against the destruction of these religious and cultural artifacts has come from other nations and people of many faiths, including Islam, but the Taliban minister of information and culture was in no mood to compromise. The remaining parts of the Great Buddhas would come down, he said, adding, "It is easier to destroy than to build."

It always is.

Tearing down is always easier than building up. Constructive action, however large or small, requires time, thought and positive action. At best, it also means respecting others, not just those who are near and dear or who are like us, but those who are not. You build up your community and your world when you show tolerance and understanding for people with whom you don't necessarily agree and who are not like you at all. You "build up" when you treat others the way you wish to be treated.

We have a name for that, of course: The Golden Rule—"Do unto others as you would have them do unto you." That rule has an honored place among the world's great spiritual traditions. Here is what various faiths believe:

Buddhism: Hurt not others in ways that you yourself would find hurtful. (Udana-Varga 5:18)

Confucianism: Is there one maxim which ought to be acted upon throughout one's whole life? Surely it is the maxim of loving-kindness: Do not unto others what you would not have them do unto you. (Analects 15:23)

Hinduism: This is the sum of duty: Do naught unto others which would cause you pain if done to you. (Mahabharata 5:1517)

Judaism: What is hateful to you, do not to your fellowmen. That is the entire Law; all the rest is commentary. (Talmud, Shabbat 3id)

Islam: No one of you is a believer until he desires for his brother that which he desires for himself. (Sunnah)

Christianity: In everything, do to others as you would have them do to you; for this is the law and the prophets. (Matthew 7:12)

Building a better world on a foundation of respect, under-standing and tolerance will never be easy, but it will always be possible. No matter how many differences we have, we have more in common. We are beloved children of God, created to love Him, ourselves and others.

And The Golden Rule, more timeless and enduring than the ancient Buddhas of Bamiyan, will continue to be the measure of humanity at its best.

Questions for Reflection

- Which rendering of the Golden Rule of the various faith traditions do you like the most? Why?

Julia's Gift

JULIA Elizabeth is my youngest niece, now fully ten years old. She is smart and beautiful. More importantly, Julia has a gentle kindness. Oh, she can be tough. Two older brothers have taught her how to be assertive. But at the heart of this young girl is a sweetness and helpfulness I treasure.

A typical image comes to mind. After shopping with my niece and nephews, we return to their home and the boys hurry in with barely a thought about helping to bring in the bags of food they will later enjoy. It is Julia who makes sure that the door is held wide open for her Uncle Jim, who is laden with all the groceries.

When the day is done, and prayers are all that stand between tiredness and sleep, Julia is attentive to pray for all those whom others might forget. She might be exhausted, but there always seems to be time for one more prayer for that very special person or intention. Julia's sweetness is also experienced through generosity. And that spirit of giving became clear, once again, in her commitment to someone she will never know.

Julia has been blessed with long, blond hair. Never cut, it runs straight down her back to her waist. People often stop her in stores to comment on her striking mane. Julia blushes a little, but not-too-secretly loves the attention. Her eyes and face shine at the mention of her beautiful tresses.

Last year Julia, who loves to read, spotted a story in the newspaper about children with cancer. The article talked about a group called "Locks of Love." This non-profit organization creates custom-fitted hairpieces for children who experience various kinds of medical hair loss. Often the chemotherapy used to treat cancer, for example, results in serious loss of hair. It's tough enough carrying the burden of illness, without also dealing with another blow to self-confidence. Approximately three hundred children have been helped so far. "Locks of Love" (1-888-896-1588, www.locksoflove.org) has arrangements with a number of hair salons to cut and style volunteers, most of whom are children. At least ten inches of hair is needed, and it takes the hair of twelve donors to make just one hairpiece for each patient.

Julia read the story and got very quiet. Minutes later she sought out her Mom and asked for permission to offer her own hair for a child in need. Julia loves her hair a lot. But she knows that someone needs it more, and she said a little wistfully, "It will grow back in time."

Listening to my sister describe Julia's decision to offer her hair made me think of the wonderful classic O. Henry story "The Gift of the Magi." It's a tale about the true spirit of giving. And it suggests that giving what we can easily do without is fine, but giving something that really matters to us means much more. I like the way Julia is giving. She gave something she loves and treasures to someone she'll never know, someone who can never say thank you. Julia already knows something about empathy. She may not know the word yet, but she certainly has the ability to imagine what it's like to go through something painful and difficult, to feel someone else's pain, and most importantly, to do something to help relieve the burden.

I love Julia's beautiful golden hair. But I love her golden and giving heart so much more.

Question for Reflection

● What marks Julia's act with the true spirit of giving?

Instruments of Peace

MARCH 1, 1961, not two months into his new administration, President John F. Kennedy brought a dream into reality. That was the date when the Peace Corps was launched. In his inaugural address, Kennedy had proclaimed: "Ask not what your country can do for you, ask what you can do for your country." But the next sentence suggested that his vision was universal. "My fellow citizens of the world," he continued, "ask not what America will do for you, but what together we can do for the freedom of man."

Kennedy realized what Pope John XXIII meant when he said that "peace begins with development." A "developed" nation, then, has food for its people, a stable yet growing economy, and the wherewithal to exist without total dependence on other nations. It is a country with real possibility. And so he initiated the Peace Corps.

Throughout my priesthood, I've met many of those who have served in this great volunteer organization. Each came to a number of new understandings about people through their experience of giving. One in particular, a woman named Gina, told me that her life was forever changed by the two years she served in the Peace Corps.

First, Gina told me it broadened her knowledge of the ways people live. Even the most seriously deprived American cannot compare to the utter poverty known by the people she served in a small town in Ghana. Gina also came to see that it was not the grand gesture, the huge food shipment or major charitable gift that mattered to people on a one-to-one basis. It was, instead, the little things done to communicate true caring. Holding a baby for the mother who was barely able to handle her two other youngsters. Bothering to struggle to learn the local language as a sign of respect for their culture.

And, finally, Gina told me that nothing meant more to people she met than a volunteer's disposition. When some Americans arrived, they'd act as if they were saviors to the down-trodden. Much as their help was, in fact, needed, these folks never truly connected with the locals. For others, like Gina, there was a connection. These were the volunteers who carried with them an attitude of gratitude. They were grateful for the chance to enter into the lives of the people they met. They appreciated the chance to make a difference for the better. "People," Gina told me, "can usually read your hearts. Especially the poor. They don't want to be an object of your pity. In fact, they resist even accepting charity they desperate-ly need when it's given from a haughty heart. But when you give with gladness, when you give with recognition that it's your privilege to serve, it makes the giving and the response not a deed of social activism. It makes it true friendship."

The Peace Corps, forty years old in 2001, was a brilliant con-cept. Sargent Shriver, its first Director, described it this way: "The Peace Corps is thousands of human beings at peace—with themselves, their fellow man, with the world. Why? Because they saved their own lives. How? By giving them-selves away."

Whether in your own neighborhood or halfway around the world, try giving yourself away. You may be surprised at how much you get back.

Question for Reflection

● Beyond the time and energy it takes to "give yourself away," what most often deters you from true servanthood?

The One That Got Away

REGRETS. If you have lived any length of time at all, you have had a few regrets. We all do. But there are some people who have a priceless ability for keeping things in perspective.

A friend told me about one of those folks. He was a man named Hugh Alexander and he died not long ago. Known as "Uncle Hughie" to generations of baseball players and executives, he was a scout, considered by many the best of all time. He had a real eye for talent, and as he traveled the country he was responsible for signing dozens of players who made it to the major leagues—athletes like Allie Reynolds, Frank Howard, and Hall of Famer Don Sutton.

Hugh Alexander was one of the most knowledgeable baseball men around. And he shared his wisdom: over the years, he taught a number of young scouts their trade. And then there was his storytelling. Alexander was known for his gift, and this is one of his favorite reminiscences.

While on one of his innumerable trips to small-town America searching for players who might have what it takes to be major leaguers, a friend gave him a name of a talented youngster. When Hugh Alexander got to Commerce, Oklahoma, he headed for the high school. He told the principal who he was and whom he wanted to see. The principal let him know that there was a problem: the young athlete had injured himself playing football and had developed arthritis in his legs.

The scout knew it was tough enough for a healthy guy to make it professionally. So when he got back to his car, he just tossed away the piece of paper with the prospect's name. Years later, Hugh Alexander said he could "still see it blowing across the parking lot."

So baseball's best scout failed to sign one of baseball's best players, Mickey Mantle.

But while he never forgot what he did, or, rather, did not do, Alexander knew better than to dwell on an error in judgment. He just got back to work and got on with life. I suspect he learned something about relying on the opinions and assessments of others without verifying them. And he just might have been reminded that we should not be too quick to judge the ability of people to overcome problems.

And, that, after all, is something his own life taught Hugh Alexander. He, too, had once been a fine young player with a bright future, joining the Cleveland Indians in 1937 when he was only 20. But in the off-season when he was working on an oil rig, a very bad accident resulted in the amputation of his hand. He could have let bitterness fill him with regret for a lifetime. But he was offered a different chance in baseball and he made the most of his life—and the most of the many lives he touched.

What about those men and women who are never able to let go of an event from the past that colors their entire lives? A bad decision or lost opportunity can gnaw away at hope and everything that makes life worth living. Whether or not you are "guilty" of something done or undone, or some tragedy strikes without your consent, you still have a choice to make. You still get to decide what your attitude will be toward yourself and the world.

You should never let your own life be the one that got away.

Question for Reflection

● Recall an event from the past that forced you to "choose life" (Deut 30:19). Where are you being called to make a choice for life today?

Listening with Compassion

MY best friend Joe was diagnosed with a brain tumor in the summer of 1999. We all knew it was not going to be a story with a happy ending, but still we tried to give Joe a sense of worth throughout his ordeal.

Before the heartbreaking day Father Joe Lukaszewski's journey ended in April, 2000, he was surrounded by moments of kindness. One gracious gift came through a simple act of listening with compassion.

From the first surgery, there was never any doubt about where he would live. We'd been friends for thirty years. He was the best I'll ever have. He wanted to be with someone who would love him without fuss or bother. He wanted to maintain his dignity with a degree of privacy. He wanted to be with someone who would protect him from well-intentioned people who might overwhelm him. I guess he knew that I'd provide him with all that because he would have done exactly the same for me. So Joe moved into my rectory.

For most of the nine months that Joe fought brain cancer, it wasn't all that hard to offer him comfort and a sense of well-being. But following the third attempt to remove the tumor, things became far more serious. Joe had lost more and more ability to communicate effectively. Words came with great difficulty. This was a deeply intelligent and intuitive man, so he knew what he couldn't do. And it frustrated him immensely.

We knew that the third surgery would probably be his last. As gently as they could, the doctors at Memorial Sloan-Kettering in Manhattan told Joe the truth: that the tumor always comes back with greater ferocity. And with its regrowth, the tumor becomes that much harder to contain or remove. So its return would be devastating. Joe had a hard time getting the right words out. He'd see an item and ask me what it was called. I wanted to keep him as communicative as possible, so I'd push him to say the word. Sometimes he'd be grateful. Other times he would be furious. But through it all, he maintained his sense of class and dignity.

Toward the end of Joe's life, maybe a month and a half before he died, we took a ride out to the countryside. We visited a restaurant we'd gone to for over fifteen years. The waitresses all knew Joe, knew that he was going through something bad. The scar on the side of his head gave proof that this was a changed man from the smiling customer they'd come to know and love over the years. Our meal was quiet, Joe couldn't speak that well. But he did notice that another priest was in the restaurant. He signaled me that a "collar" was present. He couldn't find the word for priest, but he knew I'd understand that "collar" meant priest.

The priest was a local pastor named Father Jack Sullivan. Jack spotted us, too. He waited a bit, then came to our table. In the few minutes that Jack Sullivan stayed with us, I saw one of the most telling acts of compassion I'd ever seen. Joe spoke a few sentences to Jack. Not one of which made a bit of sense. In Joe's head the words had meaning, but the tumor made communicating those thoughts nearly impossible. You would never have known that to look at Jack Sullivan's face. He nodded at Joe knowingly. He looked at him with absolute gentleness and kindness. With affirming nods and gestures, he seemed to say to Joe, "I got you, I understand." He never once made Joe feel that his language was beyond recognition. As Jack left our table, Joe was smiling. Someone seemed to understand. That understanding was a bountiful blessing.

People often think that in order to quell another's pain you have to know and say all the right words. They're mistaken. When we listen with compassion, it surmounts any and all hurdles to communication. And it gives unfathomable hope to the person in pain. I saw that glow of hope in my friend Joe's eyes that night, when a man named Jack seemed to get it. Hope offers more than life; it promises eternity.

Questions for Reflection

- Father Jack's kindness to another human being fulfills the words of Mother Teresa, "Let us do something beautiful for God." Reflect and share on the times you have been the giver or recipient of such listening.

- What makes it possible for you to accompany a loved one through a terminal illness?

All Is Forgiven

THE simplest lessons of life have a way of turning up where you least expect them. Even something as basic as learning how to say, "I'm sorry." Or, conversely, "That's okay; all is forgiven." That's just the kind of message that turned up in a recent newspaper story that appeared, of all places, on the sports page. And quite a story it is.

The story was about the blockbuster baseball trade that sent All-Star second baseman Roberto Alomar from the Cleveland Indians to the New York Mets (occasioning shouts of joy, it should be mentioned, from Met fans). All the stories in the New York papers mentioned the glowing statistics that Alomar has compiled at the plate and in the field. But on the negative side, they referred also to the unpleasant incident for which Alomar is too-often remembered: his 1996 confrontation in Toronto with umpire John Hirschbeck, which ended in an uproar when Alomar spit in Hirschbeck's face.

Most of the sportswriters took note, at least in passing fashion, of the fact that Hirschbeck and Alomar have long since settled their differences. But John Harper's story in the New York *Daily News* went a step further. He took the trouble to call each of the principal parties involved. And what emerged was a true lesson in contrition—and forgiveness.

The 1996 incident was a genuine donnybrook, one that left bad feelings all around—as sports altercations often do. There was a staged "reconciliation" handshake between player and umpire in 1996, but it was strictly for appearances. As Harper reported, Hirschbeck didn't even make eye contact with Alomar, let alone talk to him, all through the 1997 and 1998 seasons. The big breakthrough finally came in May of 1999, when a clubhouse friend whom Hirschbeck respected said some kind things about Alomar.

"That got me thinking, and I decided three years was long enough," Hirschbeck said. "I was umpiring at second base so I decided I'd say hello that night. When he came out to his position, I was about 10 feet behind him and I said, 'Hey, Robby, how you doing?' Well, it was like opening the gates. He kept turning around. He couldn't stop talking to me."

That was just the beginning. Not only did a friendship blossom, but Alomar began to help Hirschbeck regularly in fund-raising efforts to fight the disease adrenoleukodystrophy, which killed Hirschbeck's son in 1993.

Let their own words, as reported by Harper, tell the rest of the story.

Alomar: "I was surprised that night when John started talking to me . . . I'm glad he did it. I've gotten to know him and John's a great guy. I feel like he's a lifetime friend now."

Hirschbeck: "He's a good guy. We talk all the time now. I'm glad it worked out . . . It's kind of like if you have an argument with your wife. You can kind of look at each other and know it's just better to move on than rehash the whole thing. You kind of forget about it. I think he's a good person. We all make mistakes in life. If he can look back toward the end of his life and that's the worst thing he did, that's not so bad."

It's all there: Contrition. Forgiveness. And a new lease on life.

They crop up every day, these lessons for living, even on the sports pages. They're there for the taking. All we have to do is take the lessons to heart.

Question for Reflection

● Extending and receiving forgiveness are difficult acts that have far-reaching effects for the good of the world. Share a life-changing story of forgiveness from your experience.

On the Benefit of the Doubt

EVER have one of those days when you're going along, feeling fine and then somebody does something to really aggravate you?

After all, whether a driver snags *your* parking space or a co-worker infringes on *your* turf or a friend criticizes *your* child's behavior, it's their fault. There's no doubt about it, it's hard to cut other folks any slack when they are so obviously unreasonable. What is the matter with people? They can be so thoughtless. Or worse, what they're doing is so stupid and wrong, it must be intentional.

Well, maybe. When we calm down, most of us know that making mistakes is one part of being human. Here's a quote by the often-wise Anonymous that I find appropriate in a lot of situations:

When the other person acts that way, he's ugly . . .

When you do it, it's nerves.

When she's set in her ways, she's obstinate . . .

When you are, it's just firmness.

When he doesn't like your friends, he's prejudiced . . .

When you don't like his, you're showing good judgment of human nature.

When she tries to be accommodating, she's "apple-polishing" . . .

When you do it, you're using tact.

When he takes time to do things, he's slow . . .

When you take ages, you're deliberate.

When she picks flaws, she's cranky . . .

When you do, you're discriminating.

None of us want to be judged on the occasional foolish things we do, but on our overall conduct and character. We want to be given the benefit of the doubt. More than that, we want to see ourselves as open-minded and large-hearted people who are willing to offer that gift, as well.

As time goes by, though, I become more and more convinced that it is in the small everyday moments of life that we show what we are really made of. Your personality, your beliefs, your values, as well as your virtues and vices, don't just wait for a crisis or a life-changing event to come into play. And that's why we need to be generous and gentle and truthful with one another.

Alan Paton, the great South African writer who spoke and worked against apartheid for decades, wrote:

"Life has taught me . . . that active loving saves one from the shortcomings of society and the waywardness of men. . . . (Life) has taught me to seek sustenance from the endeavor itself, but to leave the result to God. To try to be free of self-deception, to try to see with clear eyes oneself and others and the world, does not necessarily bring an undiluted happiness. Yet it is something I would not exchange for any happiness built on any other foundation. There is only one way in which one can endure man's inhumanity to man and that is, to try in one's own life to exemplify man's humanity to man."

God never meant "being human" to be something we should be sorry about, but rather something to rejoice about.

Question for Reflection

● After reflecting on Alan Paton's words on life, complete your own "Life has taught me . . ." statement and share it with at least one other person.

Part II
Post 9/11

He Lived to Help People

THE Christopher message reaches out to people throughout the country and, indeed, all over the world. But our home is in New York. It always has been, ever since our founding in 1945. The people on the staff are New Yorkers—some of us by adoption, the rest of us born and bred.

That's why the events of September 11, 2001—the unspeakable attack on our city, on the men and women who were our neighbors—have hit us so hard. Of course that day's terrorism stunned the entire country and forever changed the way that all Americans live their lives. And certainly many people from other parts of the nation—far too many people—made the supreme sacrifice. But New York bore the brunt of the attack. The emotional shock and the staggering loss of life will haunt us forever.

In the midst of the horror, however, stories of heroism have emerged, helping mightily to console us in this hour of grief. Police officers and firefighters, New York's Finest and New York's Bravest, wrote many of them. So did doctors and nurses and other medical workers, rescuers, helpers of all kinds who risked their own lives trying to save the lives of others. Our own Cardinal Edward Egan rallied New Yorkers of all faiths with his presence and his words of comfort. One of his saddest duties was to offer the funeral Mass for Father Mychal Judge, a beloved Franciscan and Fire Department chaplain, killed by falling debris as he anointed a fireman at the base of one of the World Trade Center towers.

The terror of September 11, in fact, produced heroes beyond number, so many that it's impossible to tell you about all of them. So let me tell you about one. His name is Tim Stackpole, captain in the New York Fire Department. I read about Tim in a column by Denis Hamill of the *New York Daily News,* and I am confident that Denis will not mind if I share some of his fine reporting with you.

I had heard about Tim Stackpole before. In 1998, he was one of three firefighters who were swallowed into a roaring inferno when a floor gave way during a five-alarm fire in Brooklyn. Somehow, miraculously, he was rescued, along with Capt. Scott LaPiedra and Lt. Jimmy Blackmore. But all three were burned horribly. Of the three, only Tim Stackpole would survive. He came home after 65 days in the hospital and pronounced: "I'm the luckiest guy in the world. I'm George Bailey in *It's a Wonderful Life*. In tragedy, I've learned just how amazingly beautiful people and life truly are."

That would have been the time, of course, to retire on a disability pension and simply enjoy the gift of life with his wife, Tara, and their five children. Not Tim.

"It was just him," Tara Stackpole told Hamill. "It was what he loved. He lived to help people. He'd give you his heart on a plate."

Tim Stackpole went back to work. Not right away, to be sure; there were long hours, then days and weeks, of arduous rehabilitation. Then it was light duty. And finally he was back on the job, promoted to captain early in September.

He was on the job September 11. His assignment took him directly to the command center set up at the base of Tower One, World Trade Center. When that tower collapsed, Tim Stackpole was lost forever. In Hamill's words, the firefighter who came back from the dead finally gave his life for his city.

"When he got hurt in '98, he should have died," Tara said. "It was a miracle that he didn't. I believe it was part of God's plan that he'd have three more years to touch people's lives. He changed people's lives by how he lived."

Thank you, Tara, for the gift of your faith. Thank you, Tim, and God be with you forever, for the gift of your life.

Questions for Reflection

- What do you think caused Tara to see her husband's extra-ordinary recovery and then his sudden death on 9/11 as a part of God's plan?
- Recall and share the stories of other heroes you have known.

Thinking Over the Future

SOMETIMES I know why people come to talk with me. Other times it's a surprise. I've known Christian since he was a kid in elementary school. He went on to be an honors student in high school, attended a top-notch university and secured his CPA in short order. He's financially well set, engaged to be married to a lovely woman named Kim. So what, I wondered, was our talk to be about?

Christian came in looking subdued and serious. "Father Jim, you know that I always wanted to go into the world of finance. I've been blessed, I got my first job right out of grad school and I really want for nothing money-wise." As he spoke, I could sense his life plan was falling short. "September 11th really wiped me out," he said, recounting the toll of knowing young people like himself, many with little children, who were no more.

Christian recounted his experiences: attending over twenty funerals, helping to raise money for the lost firefighters and the families who now survived them, doing his part to help alleviate the suffering of too many. He was quick to point out, "I'm doing no more than millions of others. Everyone wants to do something good, something helpful. We just don't want the people who are lost to be forgotten." Everything Christian said was welcome, but not unusual. His response to this tragedy was exactly what you'd expect of people with working consciences. Then he went further.

"Those firefighters, the cops, the emergency medical service workers, they really were givers. They put themselves in harm's way because they chose a vocation of service to others. I want their life. I want to change direction. I want to get involved in a service career." Now, you'd have to know Christian to realize that this was a major departure in his life plan. Accruing money and things had always been what he termed a "successful" life. Oh, he'd give to charities. But his giving would be after profits and from the safety of a different world. The new Christian didn't want to keep a distance.

I asked him just what he was thinking about doing. He didn't know exactly, but spoke of the obvious choices, firefighter or police officer, as well as mentioning nursing or teaching as possibilities. He just wanted, he said, "to be able to say I made a direct difference for the good."

Christian's final decision might or might not mean a complete career change. Instead, he could commit some of his time and energy to volunteer work. One way or the other, I am convinced he will stay involved.

My conversation with Christian was not unique. People seem genuinely changed by the happenings of September 11th. Governor George Pataki of New York mentioned some of those changes at a dinner held in support of the families of police officers killed at the World Trade Center. "It's inspiring, and not a little bit surprising," he noted, "to see the American flag pin on lapels of people who might not have expressed such a public witness to our love of country before." And he's right. We woke up on September 12th to the reality that we have much to be grateful for, living in this free land. And when a people are blessed for many years, it sometimes becomes easy to take the blessings for granted. People seem less inclined to do that now.

We've always been grateful that some people give their lives to the service professions. Now, we see how much we need them. Just maybe, we've been awakened to the importance of living our lives, at least in part, beyond our own desires. When Christian looks to his future, it will include something done, hands on, for others. Can you imagine the world we could make if each one of us did the same?

Question for Reflection

- How has your thinking and doing been affected by the losses you experienced because of the events of September 11, 2001?

Giving Us Pause

MICHAEL Berresse, a native of Joliet, Illinois, is a star on the Broadway stage. His two biggest roles so far, have been in the hugely popular shows *Chicago* and *Kiss Me Kate.* He's also appeared in several movies, including Steven Spielberg's much discussed film *A.I.*

This talented young man is clearly on the move. He was a guest on the *Christopher Closeup* television program which taped shortly before Michael was scheduled to move to London and reprise his Tony-nominated part there as Bill Calhoun in *Kiss Me Kate.* Few members of the Broadway cast were asked to take part in the English production, but Michael's singing, dancing and amazing acrobatic skills are a marvel. Yet what most impressed me about Michael Berresse was something else entirely.

Michael should have left New York City around the time it was attacked. Instead he chose to stay. Here's what he later wrote from London: "I too was in New York on the 11th of September. I delayed my departure until the 19th so that I might find solace and hope in the connection with so many in search of a greater unity. It was incredibly powerful to see so many eyes meet mine in the streets hour after hour, day after day following the disaster. All pleading for contact. No judgment, no borders. I have never felt such grief and reverence simultaneously. It is a magnificent lesson in understanding that peace and security do not come from without, rather from within. The desire to connect is a beautiful one, but even more so when one can find the holiness and peace in that connection."

In yet another message from London, Michael spoke about the many British people who have offered support and kind words simply because he's an American. "So much sorrow and grief," he added, "and yet so much potential for growth and unity." This "potential" offers a unique opportunity.

Those stories you've heard about New York are true. In the wake of horror, people were and are different. More people now hold the door open for others. Drivers are not as consumed with bolting past the light. Cursing, swearing and mean-spiritedness are the exception. In fact, it seems not unlike the spirit you find at holiday time. Around Christmas, people who once shared only anonymity make an effort to connect. We see ourselves as members of the human family, setting aside differences and allowing for the possibilities of goodness in one another. We are not surprised when a total stranger wishes us a hearty "Merry Christmas" or "Happy New Year" for no reason except to share the goodwill or the season.

I, too, will always treasure being in New York during this time. In the midst of unspeakable tragedy, people responded with kindness, care for others, and an unexpected civility.

Most importantly, that sensitivity hasn't faded. Instead, people act as though they're in this for the long haul. September 11th changed us in so many ways—not least in giving us pause, and helping us to remember that we are sharing the human journey. The ties that bind are so much more vital than those that separate. It's as simple as this: We need each other.

The power that inspired Michael Berresse and others to stay in New York, to come here, to connect and to share with their brothers and sisters is alive and well in the U.S.A.and in the world, today. May it be a spirit that grows and prospers.

Question for Reflection

- Who were the people and places that gave you solace and hope after September 11, 2001?

Funeral Number 255

THERE were so many funerals for New York City firefighters following September 11, that the city had asked the general public to attend them wherever possible. Department members and other official mourners were being spread too thin, the city explained, because there were too many funerals to go to.

And so New Yorkers packed St. Patrick's Cathedral on November 8 for funeral number 255, just as they had been doing at other funerals since September 11. This one, it turned out, was for Firefighter Durrell Pearsall, known to his friends and family as Bronk. It was a name that hung on from his childhood, when his mother gave it to him because he was such a big boy—big, she used to say, like Bronko Nagurski, the football player.

Bronk remained big, a man of outsize proportion who celebrated life in a big way as well. He loved Irish music, Notre Dame, the cousins who formed his family, and having a good time. He especially loved being a New York firefighter. But as Father James Kissane reminded the congregation, Bronk kept it all in focus: "Bronk was a man of hope. He used his humor and his love of life to express that hope. As we gather, even in sadness, it's that hope that we must never lose."

A cousin who gave one of the eulogies said Bronk's girlfriend, Karen Jelinek, had joined him at a family gathering in August. "We knew he was getting serious about marriage when he introduced us to Karen," the cousin said. "He had never done that before. His last words to us, when he left, were 'I love you guys.' "

There were two other stirring eulogies, both given by colleagues of Bronk in Rescue 4, one of the FDNY's elite units. Lt. Mike Myers noted that the recovery of Bronk's body two weeks earlier had given family and friends a measure of consolation. When he called for the city to make sure to "bring each of these guys home," he drew a standing ovation.

"I thank God for giving him back to us," said the other eulogist, Firefighter Liam Flaherty, who also served alongside Bronk in the Emerald Society Pipes and Drums . He was a lonely kilted figure as he stood in the cathedral sanctuary, but his eloquence was stunning. Recalling a day when eight of the FDNY brothers had been recovered from the rubble at Ground Zero, he told of seeing a woman alongside the West Side Highway, holding a sign that bore a single word. That word changed his entire focus, he said, opening his eyes to "the beauty of it all."

"I saw my brothers at their absolute best, when everything, everything was at its absolute worst . . . I saw brothers work tirelessly under the most brutal conditions waving off relief, digging with their hands while being bombarded with smoke and heat . . . I saw brothers put their family lives on indefinite hold so that they could tend to the needs of their missing brothers' families . . . I saw brothers don their kilts and Class A uniforms to pay homage to our fallen at hundreds of services, tirelessly driving countless miles to make sure that each brother was sent off with the dignity and respect he deserves."

The word he saw on the woman's sign that day, he said, was "Unbroken."

Then, speaking directly to firefighters in the congregation from near and far, he called out: "Hold your heads high, my brothers. I still thank God every day that I have the privilege to work alongside great men as you. You have done our deceased brothers proud. Remain unbroken!"

The applause was thunderous.

As noted above, the funeral for Durrell Pearsall was firefighter funeral number 255. That meant there were still almost 100 more to go.

Questions for Reflection

- A sign with the single word "Unbroken" gave new hope to a distressed firefighter, "opening his eyes to 'the beauty of it all.' " What, if anything, has restored your hope?

- Recall and share your feelings about the funerals or memorial services you attended for victims of 9/11.

Hold on to Hope

MOST of the readers of this book know the Prayer of St. Francis. It's the one that begins, "Lord, make me an instrument of your peace. Where there is hatred, let me sow love; where there is injury, pardon . . . "

A prayer of breathtaking beauty and simplicity under any circumstances, it seems especially appropriate in this strange and unsettled time that has followed September 11. Not only is there comfort in its promise; its measured cadence reminds us of the things that really matter, even in the darkest days of our lives.

Consider, for example, the remaining four lines of the first stanza that was started above: "Where there is doubt, (let me sow) faith; where there is despair, hope; where there is darkness, light, and where there is sadness, joy."

Darkness and fear have surely colored the year after, and so has despair. The light of faith will always overcome fear, and as the prayer gently recalls for us, the answer to despair is hope.

As people of the Judeo-Christian tradition, we come by our hope quite naturally. It is ingrained throughout Scripture, either explicitly (as in Psalm 119, verse 49: "Remember Your word to Your servant, in which you have made me hope") or by inference. All of the Pentateuch, the first five books of the Bible, insist that divine guidance never fails, and that once we learn to follow God's way we can face life with confidence, courage, and the sure hope of God's reward.

St. Paul wrote often of the virtue of hope, and even if he assigned a greater value to that of love (1 Corinthians 13:13), he continually reminded his far-flung faithful of the role of hope in their lives—and ours. "Hope does not disappoint us," he wrote, "because God's love has been poured into our hearts through the Holy Spirit" (Romans 5:5). And again: "Continue securely established and steadfast in the faith, without shifting from the hope promised by the gospel" (Colossians 1:23).

Those last lines, particularly, might have been written for
the latter days of the year 2001. No question about it; these
were times when many were gripped by despair—and heaven
knows there was much to be desperate about. But as St. Paul
himself advises, let's not allow ourselves to be shaken from our
hope. It is through hope, after all, that we have the confident
expectation that if we hold on—persevere, endure—and trust
in God, we will get through the darkest times.

Many years ago Maryknoll Father James Keller, the founder
of The Christophers, came up with a little essay on hope that's
as inspiring today as the day it was written.

"Hope looks for the good in people instead of harping on
the worst," it begins. "Hope opens doors where despair closes
them. Hope discovers what can be done instead of grumbling
about what cannot. . . . Hope is a good loser because it has the
divine assurance of final victory."

Hold on to hope. It's a God-given gift just made for our
troubled times.

Question for Reflection

- Prayers, poems, essays and scripture abound with
  thoughts on hope. What ideas have inspired you on your
  darkest days?

It's Not What You Say

THERE'S probably no more difficult ministerial challenge than the funeral of a child. Parents are faced with a nearly insurmountable pain because the normal assumption is that their children will survive them.

When the shockingly unexpected occurs, parents' lives are upended. This wasn't supposed to happen. In meeting with the parents, as well as speaking at the wake and funeral, clergy often wonder: "What can I possibly say to these good folks? How can I offer any real comfort or solace?" In the quest to find the proper words, some ministers do very well. I've seen any number of colleagues give insight into the meaning of eternal life or articulate a personal vision of the deceased child that's warm, loving and wise. Other times, I've seen what trying too hard can do. I recall one terribly sad funeral for a teenager. He'd been driving his car in the left lane of a highway on his way to school. Another driver, in the opposite lane of traffic, lost control of her car which literally flew over the divider, squarely hitting the young man's car. He died immediately.

The funeral Mass for this well-liked young man was overflowing. All present wanted to support his parents, brothers and sisters. I could see in the face of the priest celebrating the Mass a tension, a nervousness that was palpable. He wanted to do this right, to say the perfect words of comfort, to give some meaning to this seemingly meaningless horror. For most of his sermon, he was fine. He recounted much about the young man's life, lending the talk a personal flavor that caused people to smile or cry. But he also knew that the random quality of the student's death was confusing and painful. So the priest decided to focus on the question of "why?" a little too colorfully, asking "Haven't you sometimes noticed a dog or cat killed on the road and wondered why? Why does God allow such bad things to happen to these innocent creatures?"

Now, here we were at the funeral of a vibrant young man. We didn't need the image of dead pets to give us perspective about the loss of a much-loved person. You could immediately see a look on the faces of those attending which told you the priest blew it. He overreached. He used an illustration that only distracted.

It was, for me, a classic case of trying too hard to find perfect words, a struggle that rarely ends in success. That's because there are no words that make sense of it all. It can't make sense, it hurts too much. You can be a person of deep faith, but when the heart is broken, no spiritual bromides will glue it back together.

On the *Christopher Closeup* television program, I interviewed New York City's then-Fire Commissioner Thomas Von Essen. He's the good soul who lost over three hundred of his best firefighters at the World Trade Center on September 11th. Every day for months, he'd attended funerals and memorial services. Sometimes, three or four a day. Most of those who died in the prime of their lives left behind parents, spouses, children, friends, co-workers and neighbors, who would suffer pain that is almost more than a heart can bear.

I asked the commissioner how he was able to offer help or emotional comfort. He told me something useful: no words are ever enough. Nothing you say can eliminate the hurt. Instead, you just have to be there with the people who are in pain. Love them, embrace them, cry with them and let them know you truly care. The salve you offer isn't in words, it's in presence, touch and compassion.

No one likes attending services for the dead. It's a responsibility made more difficult by our fear of what we can say to give comfort. But you can make an enormous difference for the bereaved just in being there. We have no greater gift than our caring and empathetic presence. Just go. That's enough.

Questions for Reflection

- What do you need to remember to help you overcome your feelings of inadequacy in comforting the bereaved?
- What can you say about God's role in "allowing bad things to happen to innocent people?"

On the First Day of the Week

CALLED "the holiest day of the Christian year," Easter certainly is that. It completes what Christmas starts: in December's darkness and cold, we rejoice in the birth of Jesus and His promise; in Easter's springtime, we celebrate the mystery of His death and resurrection.

The perennial liturgical cycle offers the comfort of the familiar over the course of a year. This is especially true now. Many people have had their lives turned upside down—not only the loved ones of the three thousand men, women and children killed in the September 11th attacks, but also the rest of us in America and around the world who were stunned by the horror and grief. The Christmas holidays intensified the desire for many of us to stay close to home, to be with our families, to be grateful for all we had and to mourn for what we lost.

And then we journey through Lent, so close to the suffering and dying of Christ. Easter certainly includes family gatherings, feasting on traditional foods, children in new outfits munching on jelly beans from their baskets and hunting for colored eggs. The day, at its core, is overwhelmingly spiritual. Our own mortality and the mortality of those closest to us has a new context in this celebration of life over death and eternity over time.

It isn't a coincidence that in the Gospel according to John the last miracle we see Jesus perform before He enters Jerusalem for the final time is the raising of Lazarus from the grave. The event does more than foreshadow Jesus' own rising from the dead. It shows us His deep love for a friend and for each of us as an individual. When Jesus was told that Lazarus was dying, He hesitated before going to his home in Bethany. Both Martha and Mary admonished Jesus that if He had been there earlier, their brother would not have died. Jesus responds by doing three unforgettable things.

First, He spoke to those grieving as well as to the ages when He said: "I am the resurrection and the life. Those who believe in Me, even though they die, will live, and everyone who lives and believes in me will never die." (11:25-26) Then, overcome by grief for His friend and his bereaved loved ones, Jesus wept. Even knowing what He intends to do, Jesus is still as human as He is divine, and He shows it. And, finally, they all went to the tomb: "And Jesus looked upward and said, 'Father, I thank You for having heard Me. I knew that You always hear Me, but I have said this for the sake of the crowd standing here, so that they may believe that You sent Me.' When He had said this, He cried with a loud voice, 'Lazarus, come out!' " (11:41-43)

And Lazarus did!

For two thousand years, people have probably wondered what Lazarus felt and thought in the moment he was recalled to this life. I wonder, too, but I really can't imagine. And what were his sisters and other relatives and friends going through when, in an instant, their mourning turned to joy? There are others I think about as well: on that day like every day in the history of the world, people died and others were left to grieve in the normal cycle of life and death. Until Easter morning.

For while our pain at the loss of a loved one is real, our consolation comes to us from Jesus Himself whose first words on that first day of the week were to comfort the weeping Mary Magdalene. When Jesus rose from the dead He took us with Him and broke death's power over us by exchanging time for eternity.

Question for Reflection

- How does the timeless message of Easter which we proclaim at every Mass help you to face your own mortality and that of your loved ones?

Something We All Share

IN my parish, in a suburb of New York City, the experience of 9/11 isn't just an intellectual or patriotic exercise. It's really all about people we knew and loved. You see, our community, like so many in the metropolitan area, lost neighbors, family members and friends. Our church remembers 31 parishioners who never came home that day. That's 31 families forever changed. Yet so many more feel their loss, wonder about the meaning of death and how we all cope with grief for lost loved ones.

In fact, death is a part of living. Our parish of almost 4,000 families sees at least 150 people depart each year for eternal life. And they are of all ages and backgrounds. This week alone, I celebrated funeral Masses for a couple of World War II veterans, for a 90-year-old grandmother, for an 18-year-old boy who died of bone cancer and for a 40-year-old newlywed who died in a boating accident while attempting to save his two nephews (happily, they survived).

For the believer, death represents transition, from this life to a higher level of being. For many faiths, this next life is considered a reward for the good life lived on earth. Increasingly, people speak of "heaven" as a place of endless light, joy, love and peace—a place or state of being in which serenity rules.

But what of the living? Those left behind? How are they to be comforted? How are we to cope with loss, even when a happy heaven awaits loved ones? They may be at peace, but what about us?

Here are some practical suggestions for helping ourselves and others face the inevitable reality of death:

1. There is no time line on grieving. Often enough, after the passage of a year or so, people expect the survivor to be "better," to have "moved beyond" pain. In truth, every person grieves differently. And people need to take the

time necessary to find their personal level of comfort in dealing with loss. There is simply no right time for being "over it."

2. People are pretty good about discussing the dead shortly after they depart. But people begin to embrace a respectful silence about the dead as time goes by. Don't do that! The people left behind need to talk and to hear. They need to tell and re-tell the stories of people they loved and lost. Talking about our loved ones, in laughter and tears, is the way we heal. Silence buries feelings better expressed.

3. Prayer for the dead is commonplace among many religious faiths. But sometimes it's even more helpful to pray to our deceased loved ones. If they're truly with God, then they can hear us and understand. We don't always have to talk directly to God; we can also talk with those He's called home.

4. For most folks, their greatest legacy isn't the cure of some disease or the winning of a Nobel Peace Prize. No, for most, our greatest accomplishment is family. Our family is, for many, the great "thing" we do or accomplish. Insofar as we love our families, care for our families, forgive each other and support our families, we honor those who have gone before us. When, on the other hand, we allow our families to dissolve or fall into conflict at the death of a loved one, in many ways we dishonor their legacy. Instead, make their greatest accomplishment a shining, living reality.

Many of us hope to achieve great things. But the concept of greatness is relative. I believe that one of the greatest things we can do is to love, support and nurture those in mourning. So drop by for a cup of coffee, pick up the phone, or sit down and send a note. Let those who grieve know you care. It may be just what was needed for a sorrowful soul. We have such power in being able to care. Let's use that power regularly.

Question for Reflection

● Besides offering prayers for the deceased, how can you show your love and support for those who grieve the loss of a loved one?

Part III
Relationships

Show Mom You Love Her

A FEW years ago my mother underwent heart surgery. It was a tough operation. After they rolled her into the operating room, a sensible old doctor came out and told us to go home. He'd call us when she came out of surgery. My father insisted on staying at the hospital. But my sisters and I decided to listen to the doctor.

When you're waiting for someone you love to come through major surgery time seems endless. With nothing to do but worry, my sisters and I started paging through old photo albums. And there, dating back to the 1940s and 1950s, were pictures of our parents. They looked great. My mother was beautiful and in terrific shape. We don't usually think of our parents as good-looking, because they are, after all, our moms and dads. But in page after page of the albums, we saw people of youth and zest and beauty.

Hours later the phone rang. Mom was out of surgery and we could go to Intensive Care to visit with her for a few moments. When I saw her, she looked awful, really beaten up. And the sound of the respirator drawing her breath in and out ran right through me. As I stood by her bedside, my mind was drawn back to those earlier photographs. And I wondered: what had happened to that young and lovely woman?

● Was it the burden of having children?

● Was it staying up all night with those children through measles, mumps, fevers, chicken pox, and all the other assorted ailments which plague youngsters?

● Was it the thousands of wash loads in an age before disposable diapers?

● Was it waiting for us to come home from dates, when our curfew was midnight but excuses always brought us in after 1 a.m.?

● Was it the people we dated who sometimes turned out to be every bit as bad as our parents had predicted?

● Was it the glassy eyes we averted or the alcohol on our breath (no matter how many mints we used to cover our drinking)?

● Was it our silly acts of rebellion when we rejected all authority (including our parents) as outdated and stupid and out of touch?

● Was it the vacation they didn't take because there were too many bills to cover?

● Was it all of those awful parent-teacher meetings, when teachers chided her children for unrealized "potential," but only Mom really believed that promise was there?

● Was it the times when her brothers and parents died, but there was so little time to grieve because we were children who needed to be raised?

● Was it going without so that we would have more?

● Was it the struggle to juggle the vocation of being a mother with the vocation of being a spouse?

● Was it the pain of letting go when we grew up, the challenge of loving us enough to let us be free?

Our parents give us so much, and it costs them. Our appreciation of our moms should not be limited to one day, Mother's Day. Our mothers are givers and, from time to time, we need to let them know that in a world sometimes devoid of heroes, they continue to give heroic witness.

Questions for Reflection

● What are some ways that you show/ed your appreciation for your mother for all she has done for you?

● If you still suffer from "mother wounds" speak to God about your desire for healing and wholeness.

Getting Comfortable

I LOVE seeing them a year later. My brides and grooms, I mean. One of the greatest pleasures of priesthood is the role of being witness to the weddings of so many delightful new couples.

One of the things I've noticed is the difference between the wedding day look and the first anniversary look. Frankly, they look just about as close to perfect as can be on the day they exchange vows. Generally, they've never been in better shape. The bride forsakes desserts and high calorie foods in favor of a slim waist. The groom gets to his local gym with religious fervor, and plays that last round of golf the day before, to be sure of having a tan on the wedding day. This is the routine, not once in a while, but almost always.

Millions are spent nationally on hair, nails, makeup and facials. Not to mention the costs of the perfectly tailored suits and gowns making our wedding couple stiff competition for the perfect figures on top of their wedding cake. All this and much more for one glorious day.

Then, maybe a year after they've settled in to the experience of being a married couple, you note an interesting change. They're the same, but different. Each has put on a bit of weight, often crediting the addition to the argument that "see, I can, too, cook!" Both wear comfortable clothing, a far cry from their tightly bound wedding day selves. Their color is normal, not altered by tanning salons or makeup or last minute golf outings. In short, they're not "on" but just themselves. They've learned how to relax with each other and with others. They don't need to impress anyone. And, importantly, they've come to believe that their respective spouse can and does love them as they are. Not as perfectly prepped as the wedding day, but simply as they are. It's a wonderful change to see. More so with each passing year. Dinner with couples married five, ten and fifteen years brings even greater proof of the transition. These are people who are not only comfortable in their own skins, but whose love for their partner isn't any longer based on the perfection of the "outer shell."

I recall one visit a few months ago. I remember this couple from their wedding day for many reasons. Not the least of which was the absolute perfection of their physical beauty. They were, on their wedding day, absolutely stunning. But at our recent meeting, ten years into the marriage, things had certainly changed. For him: baldness, a substantial paunch and a look of tiredness—brought on, no doubt, by ten years of commuting from suburbia to the Big Apple.

For her, those side effects of three babies included a thicker waistline and hair that needed some attention (but probably wouldn't get it, with three kids needing far more). And, again, a tiredness that comes from sleepless and attentive motherhood and being a supportive spouse—a tiredness that seemed to increase right before my eyes. And yet, and yet, the look of love, the look of being "at ease" with someone else they knew they could trust completely, was amazing to see. They had arrived at a comfort zone that eluded them before marriage. Romance, physical attractiveness and a sense of sexiness had been obvious on their wedding day. But something happened along the way. They discovered that, peel away the shell, and what do you find? A greater beauty than all the rest, the knowledge that beneath those extra pounds and changing physical looks lies a profoundly striking vision. It's the magnificence of realizing that this person is your beloved. And you are so richly blessed.

(Note: If your marriage isn't creating the comfort zone described here you may want to seek help such as Retrouvaille, which assists those with troubled marriages, at 800-470-2230, or www.retrouvaille.org)

Questions for Reflection

- What is the "greater beauty" that you see in your spouse? What keeps you from expressing to them how much of a blessing they are to you?
- What is distinct about couples who know they are blessed?

"Real" Friends

MY first parish assignment was to a church named St. Boniface. A great blend of cultures and people, it was brimming with activity. The one area that needed some work was for parishioners eighteen through thirty. So with my pastor's encouragement, I set out to establish our first young adult group. The ministry grew quickly, with members totaling nearly three hundred. Weekly meetings were packed with great people (at that time, many around my age!) who came to meet others, explore their faith and form supportive friendships. Many were at crossroads, trying to determine the purpose of life and their place in society. Many had dated and found the experience wanting. Others simply refused to believe in the reality of real or permanent love. For some, who had had a few rough relationships, marriage was a faraway notion and not for them.

Two in that last group were Mike and Nancy. Let down by love too often, they had grown cynical about the prospects of permanent commitment. Because they were a little needy and unsure of their personal value (broken hearts can do that), and given to late night conversations, they often wanted to hang out with the young priest. There were many times I found their company delightful and uplifting. An equal number of times I would gladly have paid someone to date them and give me a break!

Like most troubles or obstacles in life, their romantic crises found resolution in time. Mike discovered a great gal and, after several years of dating, married her. Nancy was equally blessed.

I mention all this because of their responses to that good fortune. Mike appreciated that he had been a slight burden during the time we'd spent together sifting through his losses in love. So when his life changed for the better, he was grateful for the attention he had gotten. Mike continued to visit, bringing his new love by to get acquainted and remaining a real friend. Mike remembered the down times and never forgot to say "Thanks for the support when I really needed it." To this day, almost fifteen years later, I regularly hear from Mike and his wife Peg. They send pictures of their children and invite me to be a part of their lives. They care about my well-being. They are there for me as I am for them.

Nancy's response was different. In her time of need and loneliness, she counted on me and others with great fervor. She frequently announced that while marriage might never happen, and romantic relationships were not to be trusted, our friendships were "for always."

Then she met a good guy. From the moment it got serious, her friends were left behind. Calls and notes went ignored. Invitations went unanswered. Nancy had finally found a true love, and the friends who nurtured her through the disappointing past no longer served a purpose.

Friendship is a precious gift. It lifts us through the times in life when we're fragile. It can help us to see the wonderful possibilities beyond our immediate sadness. Friendship is a salve that binds wounds we imagine will never heal. We're not obligated to live for our friends. But we are obligated to appreciate the good they do for us in our hour of need because real friendship is never one-sided.

Who are those who have sustained you in the dark times? Have you returned the favor? Have you said thank you? Today would be a good time to remember and to be the friend you would want to have.

Questions for Reflection

- Let today be the day to ask these important questions (in the last paragraph) and to be the friend you want to have.

Love Is Greater

IT was about twenty-five years ago that I attended Colleen and Jack's wedding. I was a relatively young guy, but couldn't mistake the passionate feelings these two shared for each other. They were the couple you just know will accomplish everything. And for a while, they did. Jack was a huge success on Wall Street. Colleen was the perfect homemaker, and in short order, the perfect Mom. They had a family of five children—not surprisingly, all great kids. So here they are: rich, beautiful, strongly attracted to each other, parents of wonderful children, liked and respected by many in the community.

Then, for no reason in particular and for many reasons, Colleen and Jack start to drift apart. Work consumes him; the family consumes her. They spend less and less time focusing on each other. He takes more trips without his wife. She finds new friends with whom she shares intimate details of life. He uses alcohol as a release. Her relationships with other men go beyond appropriate boundaries. The children watch sadly as Mom and Dad come home more angry after marriage counseling than before.

In the midst of pain and poor communications, Colleen takes a boyfriend. Jack finds out and files for a divorce. Our perfect couple now see each other very differently. To Colleen, Jack was the bully she never really liked nor respected. He drank too much. He noticed too many younger women. He dumped responsibility for the children on his wife.

Jack's viewpoint has also changed. Colleen kept a messy home and rarely cooked a decent meal. The children got away with too much. She was a permissive role model who gave them too much freedom. She took up smoking pot, even at home! And the final straw: she cheated on her husband—though he never mentioned that he'd given into temptation a few times himself.

The divorce comes, ugly and painful. As Danny DeVito's character wisely admits in the film *The War of the Roses*, "In divorce, there are no winners, it's only about degrees of losing." And so it was for Colleen and Jack, two scarred people who could see little good in their children's other parent.

And then it happened. The youngest child, Brendan, is in a terrible accident. He survives, but is disabled for life. Left without the use of his legs or arms, the former athlete needs his family now more than ever. Jack and Colleen, along with their other four children, respond with enthusiastic and loving support. Suddenly, the issues and mistakes that divided a home don't seem so important when measured by the love and healing given Brendan in his time of need. I saw these two divorced parents at the hospital, in follow-up therapy and many times since that awful accident. They look at each other with renewed respect and appreciation. You can almost see love again.

No, they won't be getting re-married. But they will remain friends. They will, once again, share conversations of intimacy and caring. Because Jack and Colleen have learned a valuable lesson borne of pain: that in any close relationship love may change and evolve. It may ebb and flow. Yet there is much more to love than you see. The differences, the battles, the hurts, the betrayals are important. But nowhere as powerful as generosity and reconciliation, never more lasting than forgiveness and redemption.

Question for Reflection

- What have you learned from enduring or witnessing a love relationship that changed?

Going to Church

I WAS heading over to church one Sunday morning to help with Communion. When I got to the sacristy, I realized that the priest celebrating Mass was just completing his homily. So I decided to take a step outside to enjoy the pleasant weather.

As I went out a side door I bumped into two sheepish teenage guys who were leaving. They clutched in their hands copies of the parish bulletin: parental notification of the fact that they had been to church. "Busy day?" I asked them. "No," said the older boy, "we're just bored." They mumbled good-bye and took off.

Watching the two of them retreat, I started thinking about some of my own friendships over the years—and the elements that make those relationships work. It certainly isn't excitement: friends sometimes bore each other. It isn't intellectual: sometimes our conversations are dull beyond belief. It isn't the richness of our personalities: we can be annoying, obnoxious and difficult to be around. It isn't power or money: we haven't got much. In fact, it's less a "feeling" of friendship than a commitment to be friends: our desire to be loyal and our decision to be there for each other.

And friendship, I think, is at the heart of our spiritual lives, too. Sometimes going to church can be boring, dull and intellec-tually vacant. And if we're expecting exciting entertainment, we will surely be disappointed. Rather, we are there because our friend God has invited us to be there. If we are true friends, we take that invitation seriously. That means we reject all the non-sense we use as excuses for staying away, like:

"I'm really busy." There are 168 hours in every week. We somehow find the time to eat, to sleep, to go to school or work, to play sports or pursue hobbies, to be with people we care about, to take care of a great number of personal obligations and preferences. In fact, we find the time for everything we really believe is important. If our God and His people are important to us, we will also make the time to be there.

"But the sermons are so boring." Give me a break. If we switched off everyone and everything that's boring in life, we would stay home in bed. Assume the speaker is trying hard. Shouldn't we try to listen? And more to the point: we are not just there for the homily. We go to be part of a community that needs us. We go to get closer to God, who never bores us or gives up on us.

"I can find God in many places. I don't need a church to pray." That's true. But let's be honest: if we don't go to church, how much serious praying do we really do? And further, where else can you go to receive Communion? Are they giving It out someplace else? More importantly, Jesus told us in no uncertain terms: I want you to gather with other believers to celebrate My life.

"I used to go, but I had a really bad experience at church." We have all had some bad experience at church. But again, let's compare our experience of God's friendship with the rest of our lives. If every time we had a poor experience with our parents, siblings or friends, we said, "That's it, this relationship's over," we would have none at all. But we keep working at relationships that matter. We forgive, we compromise and we try to love again.

If we give the same energy to our love of God and His people as we give to our friends and family, maybe we would find that the boredom that put us off wasn't really inside the church, but inside us. And that's something we can change if we are willing. After all, it's for a Friend.

Question for Reflection

- What makes you say "yes" to God's invitation to go to Mass, even when you're busy, bored, tired or angry with what's going on in the Church?

Another Word for Love

MICHAEL was my cousin. We were born a year apart. And as I have two sisters, he was—for a time—like a brother to me. Being a year older made him feel protective of me. We lived in Brooklyn, and Michael was an intuitive street kid. He had smarts about real life I couldn't even begin to have. Michael was cool. He knew the deal. I admired him. He was also talented, not in an academic way, but with an ability to read people. He was sensitive. He was funny. He could be very kind. He was handsome. He was charming. He could get you to believe that whatever he said was the absolute truth. Even if it was a lie.

During high school, Michael and I started to head down different roads. He got involved with a world that was foreign to me. He drank a lot; did drugs a lot; fooled around a lot. Sometimes he got burned.

His parents, his teachers and some of his friends challenged him to pull it all together. But he was an unbelievable con-man. He would look you in the eyes; tell you that drugs and alcohol were the worst; swear he was finished with them; get you to smile supportively—and be stoned the next day.

This went on for years. And the truth is that we all knew that he was full of it. But we wanted to believe in him so much that we accepted what we should have rejected. I can remember many occasions when I'd be sitting with Mike and asking him about how his "problem" was coming. And he would, as always, assure me that things had been bad, but now he was really on the right track. Once, he even gave me some of the pills he'd been addicted to. "Throw them out," he said. "I wanna be clean again." I bought the act only to find out that what he'd given me was only a fraction of what he had. And, you know, deep down I always knew he was lying. But it's so hard to say that. It's so difficult to look at people you love, listen to their stories and blow them out of the water by telling

74

them that you're not buying a word of it. Maybe I wanted to keep Michael's love and friendship more than I needed to expose the unspoken truth.

One day, several years ago, the lies caught up with Michael. He got up in the middle of the night and took into his body more than it could handle. He overdosed, and died within hours.

His death devastated us all. We should have seen it coming, but I guess we denied the inevitable. Our feelings during the wake and funeral were all jumbled. We were angry about drugs. We were angry with Michael. We were angry with God. And if we were really honest, we'd have to admit we were most angry with ourselves. Because, deep down, we believed that we could have done more.

A few weeks ago, right in the rush of the Christmas season, I paused to think about what it really means to be with the people we love. Partying with them, eating with them, going to church with them, giving gifts to them, are all important and good. But we also need to use our times together—throughout the year—to tell each other the truth. Even truths that make us uncomfortable or angry.

My memories are often of Michael. I miss him, I loved him, and I wish I had loved him enough to say "stop."

Whatever the person you love is doing—drugs, drinking, sex, lying, cheating, stealing, or putting people down—it's a true sign of caring to confront and to challenge. Real friends aren't the ones who tell us "yes, yes, yes." Our truest friends may have to say "no." For "no" can be, an expression of love, too.

Questions for Reflection

● What has been your experience in confronting someone you love with the truth? Is there anything you would do differently now?

Between Parent and Child:
Facing Hard Truths

YOU never forget your first car. I remember every detail about mine. It was a Chevy Nova, sky blue and beautiful. I was in college and couldn't afford it without financial help from my parents. Their only condition was that I drive carefully. Not two months after I got the car, disaster struck. I was heading home far too late from a high school reunion. I remember thinking: it would be nice just to close my eyes and rest for a second. My next memory was seeing my car wrapped around another car. Nobody, thank God, was hurt. But the Nova was history.

It took me a day to call home. My mother was understandably upset. My father was away on business and she suggested I call him. "That won't be necessary," I said. "I'm not telling Dad about the accident." I don't remember exactly what my mother said, but the gist of it was: it's going to be kind of hard to explain the missing car over the next few years.

She was right. I had to come clean and tell him. But I was sure my father would lose it and chew me out and that he'd never trust or help me again. I felt like a frightened, stupid fool. Three days after the conversation with my mother, with a knot in my stomach, sweaty palms and a tension headache, I called my father and broke the news. Long pause. Dad asked, "Was anyone hurt?" "No." "All right, all right, relax, we'll talk about it when I get home," was all he said. That was it. No screaming, no put-down, no "How could you be so stupid?" Just concern coupled with the relief that no one had been hurt.

Many young people sell parents short, seeing their limitations and not their strengths. Parents often misjudge themselves, too. They may have no idea how great their coping skills are—until they are most needed.

I had a visit one day from a young couple who had been dating for about a year. Something was making them tense.

Finally, Valerie broke the news: "Father Jim, we're pregnant." I was happy for their expected child, if not thrilled with the circumstances, but there were more problems. "Look, Father, Kevin and I love each other and we believe that it is wrong to get rid of the baby." I, obviously, agreed. "But Father, if my parents find out that not only were we having sex, but that I'm pregnant, they'll kill me."

This was not the first time I'd heard about "parents who'd never understand." In most high schools I visit, the very first reason students give for why they'd abort is the fear of telling their parents the truth. Parents become the fall guys in this difficult situation. So I proposed to Valerie that I would go with them to break the news. She agreed, and later that night we arrived at her parents' home. Her father was warm and welcoming. But in the next half-hour the tone of the visit changed.

True to Valerie's predictions, her father went crazy when faced with the news. He yelled, cursed and called her a slut. He promised to throw her out of the house. Meanwhile, her mother cried, and her boyfriend Kevin just kept quiet. After hours of hysteria, we called it a night. Valerie's dad stayed angry for about a month. But he did not throw her out of the house and, gradually, he came around. He started to drive Valerie to the doctor, he nagged her about eating right, and he complained about her smoking, because "it would hurt the kid."

When little Vanessa was born, I had the privilege of baptizing her. When the christening was over, I stood at the door of the church to say good-bye. The person who lovingly cradled this beautiful baby in his arms was Grandpa, his eyes bright with tenderness. For beyond the anger, confusion and pain of seeing his daughter make a mistake, he was what all good parents strive to be: loving, compassionate and resilient.

"Coming clean" may not be easy for adults or young people. But it's almost always better—for everyone.

Questions for Reflection

- Describe an incident which dispelled the fear that "they'd never understand." Is there anyone who you need to "come clean" with?

- What are the advantages of "coming clean"?

More Than You Know

I'M in my office and a young woman comes in to talk. She's about twenty-four years old and badly shaken by the recent death of her father. We speak about the meaning of life and death. She particularly wants to know about the afterlife. What, she asks, is heaven really all about? How can we know that it exists? How can a person enjoy a happy life beyond this life? What kinds of sin would keep a person from experiencing God's goodness and mercy in the life-to-come? Now that someone she loves has died, Marianne needs to know. And she wants, more than ever, to be a person of faith. She wants to believe in the transcendent. She wants to believe in a life greater than our earthly existence. But sometimes hope fails her. Sometimes she's paralyzed by doubt. Sometimes it's too hard to believe in a reality you can't taste or see or feel.

Toward the end of our encounter Marianne looks sad. Her words revealed her struggle. "Father Jim, I wish I could be more like you. I wish I could believe that my father is more alive now than he was before. Believe me, no one wants to trust that there's a heaven more than me. But I just can't. My faith is so weak." Marianne is not alone. Many people I know and love are unsure of their faith. In a world that celebrates the provable, the verifiable and the scientific, belief in that which we cannot confirm seems too hard by half.

Maybe we're being too hard on ourselves. Maybe we're more given to faith than we know. Maybe we do, in fact, trust the unknown more fully than we realize. An example: after generations of talk about the supremacy of science over belief in God, polls tell us differently. One survey, published recently in *Parade* magazine, has over 90 per cent of the American people saying they believe in God.

Perhaps more convincingly, are the signs of faith all around us. Think of them. You drive your car and stop for a traffic light. You trust that when it's green for you, it's simultaneously red for those in the cross traffic. You have no way of knowing if that's true, but you trust nonetheless.

You travel to see relatives in another state. You board an airliner. You sit in a seat and allow someone you don't know and never met to lift you and the others around you to a height of thirty-five thousand feet. You put your very life in the hands of a stranger who, you believe, will get you there in one piece.

You go to a doctor and essentially place your body in his or her hands. You trust them to know their business. You don't know if the day they operate is a good or bad day for them. You rarely know the statistics on their rates of success. But they're doctors and you tend to believe they can make it all right.

Or how about love? You date a person for a while. You think you've come to know them. Together you decide to build a life together. The marriage takes place at which you promise before God to love, honor and respect each other always and forever. You don't know what the future holds. You don't know how well or how poorly the two of you will handle the inevitable disappointments and challenges of life. In so many ways, every act of love and commitment, every marriage is a leap into the unknown. But you take the chance. You accept the challenge. You dare to make a leap of faith.

In each case, you accept risk. You decide that some things that cannot be seen or proven must be left to faith. I think most of us believe far more than we know. We recognize at some powerful inner level that life is without meaning unless it's lived with hope and trust. Marianne thought she was weak in the ways of faith. But her search, her questioning and the very act of loving her Dad showed something else. It demonstrated that we are, by our very nature, given to trust. We are, thank God, people of faith.

Questions for Reflection

● Have you ever been paralyzed by doubt? How did you work through it?

Rectory Living

ONE of the last mysteries of life in the Church may concern the place priests live, the rectory. Unfortunately, because of the diminishing number of priests, many live alone. But in the popular imagination, we're still perceived like Bing Crosby's Father O'Malley in the classic film *Going My Way*, where several priests share their living space. In fact, that's what my rectory is still like.

We are three priests, each with his own living room, bedroom and bathroom. We share a common kitchen, dining room and communal living room. On the first floor of the rectory are our parish offices. Each priest has an office for counseling, planning weddings with engaged couples and just meeting people to talk.

Also sharing space with us at the rectory from nine to five are the parish secretary and receptionist. These are the front line people who field the calls that come in, provide information, make sure the weekly bulletin is published and handle our parish website (www.stthomasapostle.org). More and more people join the parish or seek help online. It's a whole new approach, and opens our parish to a world of visitors.

Down one corridor is the bookkeeper's office. She works with a top-notch finance committee made up of parish laypeople who work in the financial field. It's amazing to think that pastors once made money decisions alone. What a blessing it is to have people who understand financial planning as principal collaborators.

In the basement are meeting rooms for every kind of group and organization. On different nights, you'll find the parish liturgy committee, the pastoral council or the local AA group using that space. Just down the hall is the Parish Social Services ministry. There, folks who are having a tough time can find practical and material help. We provide food, clothing, diapers or even a month's rent, depending on the need.

That's the basic layout. But let me talk about living there. Rectories are much like any home. Priests eat, talk and socialize together. In one of my earlier jobs, I had to travel to a different parish each weekend. I'd usually stay over on a Saturday night. Joining my brother priests for dinner was always revealing. In some places, conversation and laughter would flow and the meal would go on and on, making it like any enjoyable family supper. In other rectories, you sensed that the guys couldn't wait to finish eating. Depending on the group dynamics and individual personalities, you could feel the tension. Dinner would be over in a half hour or less, each priest quickly returning to his private quarters to watch television alone. Those rectories were sad to visit. When I became a pastor myself, I remembered those unhappy visits and promised myself that I'd try to create a happy home for the priests I was assigned to live with. How? Well, it's not unlike any family home.

First, there needs to be collaboration. No one member of the house has all the answers, so we need to be open to others and their ideas. Second, we are all different. We see truth in personal ways, but every point of view is worthy of respect and a fair hearing. People who are not listened to tend to become hurt and embittered. Third, it's important to have fun together. The guys in our home do more than just work together; we make time to go out as a group. It may just be to a movie or a dinner, but it's a sign that we enjoy relaxing as well as working together. Fourth, individual TV-watching can make a very solitary existence. We have a TV and VCR in our communal living room and watch occasional programs together. Finally, it's always important to pray together. It may be something as short as grace at meals, but it reminds us that everything we have is the Lord's.

The rules for happy and healthy rectory living are really not unlike the rules for good family living. They're not complex, but they do help to create a more harmonious community.

Questions for Reflection

- What are the greatest barriers to good family living for you?
- Is it easy for you to think of rectory living in the same way as the family next door?

Close to Home Heroes

I WAS called recently to officiate at the funeral for a high school classmate's Dad. He was a true nobleman, his father, always doing for others. Jim Nevins not only went to church regularly, he also put his faith into action. There are countless families, down on their luck, who had occasion to seek his help through decades of service in the St. Vincent de Paul Society. He never turned his back on anyone.

At home, Jim faced his own challenges. He had a beloved daughter in a difficult marriage. After three beautiful babies arrived, her husband walked out. Jim Nevins and his equally devoted wife welcomed their daughter and her children into their home.

The Nevinses put aside their own longtime plans and got on with the business of raising a new generation of children. I know from my classmate Tom, the uncle to these three children, that the going was not always easy. Children are the greatest miracle in the world, but they don't come with instructions. You learn by doing, and sometimes that includes mistakes. The key is faithfulness, being there through the valleys and mountaintops of daily living. Jim Nevins was there for those children, always.

At the funeral service, one of those children, now a grown and married man in his twenties, got up to speak. His name is Jonathan and his words were simple, eloquent, and powerful testimony to the power of one life well lived for others: "In so many ways, my Granddad was the only real father figure I had. Everyone talks about love in the family. His was real. In fact, it was unconditional. For a long time I think we just thought that's the way it's supposed to be. Didn't realize how great was his giving, his sacrifice for us."

Jonathan continued, "For a lot of my life, I looked for heroes. In my teenage years, the heroes were mostly professional athletes. Their power and success, the adulation they enjoyed, made them bigger than life. They were my heroes for a time. Then as I got older and more career oriented, I came to admire money and those who made a lot of it. So people like Bill Gates became my heroes.

"Recently, watching my grandfather struggle with illness, I got focused on what really makes someone a hero. And remembering my grandfather's devotion to us, his self-sacrifice, his great sense of humor even in difficult times, his absolute, and always freely-given love, I realized who my truest hero is. It's my Grandpa."

So many of us seek someone special to emulate, to admire, to look to. Maybe we look too far. There could be some truly remarkable people close to home, if we only have the eyes to see. Sometimes they come in the form of stooped and wrinkled figures. Sometimes those worn out bodies hide hearts of radiant gold.

Jenny, Jonathan's sister also spoke that day. Her eulogy took the form of a poem:

"You are in my heart, Grandpa
No matter where I am
You are to me like
A warm and bright sunshine amidst the cloudy gray
A spot of colorful joy that doesn't fade away
Rising in me and through me
And our whole family eternally.

Faithfulness and love leave their own legacy. Jim Nevins, rest in peace.

Question for Reflection

● Is there someone in your life whose legacy of faithfulness and love you want to eulogize?

Love Made Real

BROADWAY is alive and prospering, with thousands of people from around the world coming to the Big Apple each day to enjoy theater in its many forms: dramas, comedies and musicals. Some of the most popular shows are musical revivals. People admire and respect the new and innovative. But they glory in tunes they know and remember as echoes of their own past.

One big audience favorite is Meredith Willson's *The Music Man*. The story of con man Harold Hill and his magical effect on River City, Iowa, never seems to age and continues to captivate young, old and everyone in between. In the recent production, Hill was played first by Craig Bierko and later by Eric McCormack. To their great credit, both held their own in giving terrific interpretations—no easy task when you're up against the stunning memory of Robert Preston, who introduced the role first on Broadway and then starred in the movie version. Marian the Librarian, the female lead, was played in this production by actress Rebecca Luker, who interprets songs like "My White Knight" and "Till There Was You" as if she were born to the part.

Sometimes, even when you know a song or a scene like the back of your hand, it can strike a new, revealing note. It happened to me during a performance, not once but twice. I experienced new insight into human love at its best. Let me tell you about it.

Near the end of the play, Marian and Harold are coming to realize how deeply they care for each other. She sings "Goodnight My Someone," while he responds with the classic "76 Trombones." In fact, they are basically the same tune, though the words and tempo are different. In the middle of this impressive duet, they switch lyrics. Her song becomes his, and vice versa. In that moment they reveal one of the great truths about real love. It grows most potent when we share each other's vision. Now, there's nothing wrong with a couple remaining the individuals they are even in the midst of a deeply loving relationship. But how powerful is love in which they're able to mutually sustain each other through a shared vision. It's a magical revelation of the very meaning of love.

Another, different image of love comes moments later. The townspeople call Harold Hill a fraud because, lacking any knowledge of music, he cannot teach their youngsters to play the instruments he has sold them. Bravely supporting their much chastened "instructor," the children attempt a few discordant notes. Horrible as they sound, the parents of these same children are thrilled. To them, this dissonant music is the sweetest of sounds. The theatrical moment is filled with truth. We appreciate people we really love well beyond their abilities. That's because we aren't looking for perfection, we're looking just to see them try. And their trying is our delight. The parents of River City don't hear music which is technically proficient, they hear magnificent music because it's played by their children!

That's exactly what love does. It lets us see and hear our beloved through a wonderfully personalized prism. As a priest, you see these eyes and ears of love in so many moments. A bride walks down the aisle in church. She's attractive, yes, but look into the eyes of her groom or her parents and you'd think they were seeing the world's most radiant vision. For them, she is.

Looking at life through the eyes of love can transform us. Perhaps that's because our sight becomes God's own: His vision can only be loving and His people can only be beloved.

Question for Reflection

● When is listening with the ear of the heart and looking with the eyes of love most difficult for you?

Through the Years

MY folks met in a Brooklyn park sixty years ago. My dad was playing softball. My mother was with friends. On that sunny afternoon they struck up a conversation. They began to date and decided to marry. But those plans were postponed by the Second World War. Separated for most of four years, they nonetheless maintained the only lifeline open to people in love back then. They wrote letters.

Happily, those letters survive today and tell a story of long distance love. Not an easy love to maintain, but one they nurtured regardless. Ending the war as a Marine captain, my dad came home and they finally married. He became a New York City police officer and detective. She kept busy with the three of us youngsters. I gather that life was happy, but also a struggle, especially when he decided to go to law school. Through child rearing and tight money, through the move to suburbia and the loss of loved ones, they kept on living out their love.

Now here's the most recent chapter. Mom underwent what should have been fairly routine surgery. Dad was with her, just planning to sit by her side and do his crossword puzzles. Before his eyes, he saw my mother collapse. Doctors and nurses came quickly, thank God. In the middle of their efforts to save her life, I called the hospital room. Imagine my surprise when a nurse asked who I was. "I'm her son," I replied. My dad then came to the phone and told me: "Your mother has collapsed. Come quickly."

I have no recollection of the road that day. By the time I arrived, the doctor had brought her back to a modest stability. But we counted our blessings prematurely. As they moved her to Cardiac Care, she went back into seizure. A second Code Red was sounded. Again, that team of experts did what never ceases to amaze me. But this time they had one problem they hadn't counted on. It was my dad. After her first attack, my mom had weakly told my father "please don't leave me." Well, he took her at her word. No doctors or nurses were going to move him. He parked himself within inches of my mom and stood watch as the doctors did their best. And their best was incredible. They brought her back a second time, got her stable and, in time, sent her home. My father's tenacious loyalty continues. He is her primary caregiver. He's positioned a couch next to her bed so that he can be there in the night. The nurses and therapists they have know that they need to work with the person who guards her with tenderness: her partner, her oldest friend. Her husband.

Recently, after tending to her from dawn, Dad fell asleep at the dining room table. So we let him sleep. I mentioned to my mom that Dad was obviously tired. She nodded and then said something that will always stay with me. "You know, Jim, we've been through so much in a lifetime together. The war. The children. The tough years. The loss of our parents and brothers and sisters. But after fifty-six years of marriage I can honestly say, I've never felt closer to your dad than I do now. He has been so caring, so patient, so good."

Tom Brokaw has written a wonderful book about the generation who fought and won the Second World War. He rightly names them *The Greatest Generation*. They accomplished amazing things. But I think their greatest feats continue to be lived today. In the faithfulness they share. In the devoted care they offer. In living out promises made so long ago, our folks teach us so much. In their lives, we are so richly blessed.

My dad was a courageous Marine, a dedicated police officer. he was a terrific lawyer and teacher. But, for me, the greatness of his caring at home is a quality that matches or surpasses what we do in our public lives. Loving for the long distance, now that's something to be proud of!

Question for Reflection

● Relate a "love in action" experience that you witnessed in your family. Acknowledge this loving act by either telling the person or praying to them if they are deceased.

Part IV
Hard Decisions

Hard Decisions All Around

THERE'S no doubt that life can be complicated, if not down-right messy. That certainly applies to the spiritual and moral decisions we are called on to make. You have to make them, just as I do, just as bishops and celebrities do—which brings me to these thoughts.

Like many people, I have long enjoyed Anthony Quinn's films, from *Zorba the Greek* to *Shoes of the Fisherman*. So, a while back, I was glad to meet him. He was rather quiet, respectful, hardly the larger-than-life character he often portrayed. With him was his wife, Kathy Benven. She had been his personal assistant. They fell in love and had children. Faith was important to her and she wanted to marry in the Catholic Church. Quinn's first wife had died and he and his second wife had married civilly, so the possibility existed. But he also had a reputation for well-pub-licized affairs. And Anthony Quinn had a history of disliking what he viewed as pretense in the official Church. Born a Catholic, he wandered a wide spiritual road.

When he died not long ago, his wife wanted final services at the Cathedral in Providence, Rhode Island. That diocese has an extraordinarily kind and pastoral shepherd, Bishop Robert Mulvee, who faced a sensitive situation, one many face in parish life. When someone has not been active in his or her religion, who has even spoken critically about aspects of the faith, is it right to grant a Mass of Christian Burial?

I happened to be visiting Bishop Mulvee about that time and he told me that he had no objection to a priest being present at the burial. But he was unsure of the wisdom of a large funeral Mass at the Cathedral on behalf of someone who seemed disin-clined to either receive the sacraments or be otherwise involved in the life of the Church. Here is a diocese that wants to respect the deceased and his family, but also wants the sacraments to be celebrated by those who honor them; a diocese that sees a funer-al Mass celebrated in the Cathedral as a public statement of honor which the deceased may not even have sought.

This situation raises the issue of the Church's sacramental life. Is it open to all, even those who seem to have left their religious identities behind? Or should comforting the grieving survivors take precedence?

Often, in a parish, you meet folks who haven't been near a church in years. They come to baptize their child. Or for the child's preparation for First Communion or Confirmation. For some, it's the first time they've been in touch since they got married. For others, who weren't married in the Church, the last point of contact may be even longer. I know that some priests have serious and understandable reservations about families that want to celebrate the sacraments for their children but who have not had—and probably will never have—an ongoing relationship with the Church. Other priests see it differently. They reason that rejecting a family's desire for a child to be welcomed to the sacraments is a sure way to make them former members of the Church—permanently.

Then there are the families with loved ones who have died, people who began life as Catholics, but wandered. This is not a battle between the bereaved in need of comfort and a hardhearted hierarchy. Rather, we have a family which seeks to honor the dead and a shepherd who seeks to protect the dignity of the sacraments. There are no bad guys here. Only people with a decidedly different vision of the proper role of the Church.

We live in a culture where verbal battles fill TV and radio, and demonizing different points-of-view is almost the norm. Yet, take a moment for reflection. Isn't it possible that we can live comfortably with a variety of opinions, without calling into question the integrity of those with whom we disagree?

Question for Reflection

● What do you consider to be a fair and just way to resolve differences with those whom we disagree?

The Knowing Parent

BILL Gildersleeve was on the line in front of me at the grocery store last week. He wasn't alone. His two little daughters, who looked to be eight or nine years old, were helping Daddy shop. Well, adding things to his shopping cart might be more like it.

Checkout lines must be designed by someone who likes to torment parents. The assorted temptations on display include tons of candy, toys and magazines. So here you have it: a parent's just finished trekking up and down the aisles, trying to balance what's needed and what's affordable and then it starts. The children see something at checkout they just "have to have." Well, not really. But they want it anyway. Say no, you're likely to face protests and griping. Say yes and you've given in to the manipulations of both children and store owners. So what are you to do? My friend on the line faced a similar dilemma.

Now, before sharing Bill Gildersleeve's response to his children, let me tell you about the man. In our town, he has always been the local star, the fellow who had it all. With looks, popularity and a lovely wife, his life looked to be a gift. He was also blessed with a natural entrepreneurial spirit. He knows business and what people want. Put simply: Bill is the image of success. But parenthood's a different game. Success in sports, business, school is absolutely no assurance that you'll be a great parent. That's the job for which there is no training: you learn by doing. Frankly, most parents would admit that they make lots of mistakes along the way. So I watched Bill and his girls with no little interest. How would this guy handle the minefield of demanding youngsters? From where I stood, Bill hit a home run. He didn't say yes and he didn't say no. He calmly listened to their requests and quietly said: "Not this time, perhaps next time." And, amazingly, they nodded, they understood. He hadn't rejected the idea out of hand. He just wasn't acquiescing right now.

No one likes being told "no." Whether you're eight or eighty, we like to hear the word "yes." We want it our way. There are very few ways that "no" won't be taken as a form of rejection. What Bill did was to listen first, then qualify his answer. That is a much more respectful way to handle people of all ages.

For example, if you tell me your opinion and I immediately say, "No, you're wrong," there's no way you're going to be open to my alternative point of view. But if, on the other hand, I listen to you respectfully and then respond by affirming what you said and yet expressing a different view, it will go down much better. Now my point may be diametrically opposed to yours, but I bet you'll at least listen and consider what I'm saying. Why? Because I respected you and your thoughts well enough to affirm and consider what you said.

Communication is the key to bridge-building. In a world with deep rivers of misunderstanding and mistrust, we need every bridge. And we build them by communicating our truth gently and showing real consideration for the other person and for his or her viewpoint.

That's what I think happened in the grocery store last week. Bill Gildersleeve didn't just say no, he opened a door to possibility. His daughters knew they were heard. They nodded and helped him carry the bags of groceries to the car. I guess Bill has found success, too, in the place it matters most, in his family. Whether between family members or strangers, respect is always the best place to start.

Question for Reflection

● How has Bill's example helped you in dealing with similar dilemmas?

The Gift of Letting Go

BILL LaRousse is a sensational guy. We attended college together and he was someone admired and liked by most. I can't remember a bad word spoken about the man.

Sadly, in our freshman year, Bill's dad died. His already close ties to his mother Mary and his brother Lloyd were only strengthened. The loss seemed to make them even more aware of their need to be a close-knit family. But after college, Bill decided that he wanted to follow in the footsteps of his Uncle Walter, a Maryknoll missioner who for many years has served some of the world's neediest people. Now, Bill is a Maryknoll missioner too, and for most of the past twenty years he's been a source of faith and practical assistance to the people of the Philippines. He rarely gets home but communicates with his Mom and brother often.

I respect Bill's choice of ministry immensely. It demands a special gift, that of detachment, the ability to step away from what we love for the sake of a greater good, or a more profound need. There's no doubt that Bill loves his family, but there is even less doubt that his presence in the Philippines has made an incredible difference for the good.

Chris Cardone is a Dominican priest. He, too, was a local boy loved by all who knew him. Chris chose to leave a privileged life, strong family ties and personal popularity to become a missionary in the Solomon Islands. On his infrequent visits, Chris comes back looking thin and tired, even sick with malaria. But I've never seen him unhappy. In fact, comfortable as his R-and-R may be, he always gets antsy after a while. He wants to get back to the people he loves and serves. In recent years, Chris's family and friends have hoped that his assignment would end, and that he'd come home to be the son, the brother and the uncle they've been missing. Then, just as that looked possible, things changed dramatically.

Chris was selected to become a bishop for the people of the

Solomon Islands. Now, every priest offered the chance to be a bishop can refuse it. In this case, you might think that was a real possibility. After all, agreeing to being a missionary bishop means that we are not likely to see Chris Cardone back home on any permanent basis until he's ready for retirement. But "yes" is exactly the answer Chris gave, though it came with great personal sacrifice. At the Mass held to celebrate Chris Cardone's elevation to the episcopacy, no moment was more tender than the one in which he thanked his parents. That emotion-laden acknowledgment recognized that in choosing to serve, he may never again live in his parents' homeland.

Bill LaRousse and Chris Cardone have made a choice to be people of detachment: people who love their families deeply, but love the call to help God's larger family even more. Theirs is a life of sacrifice and of self-giving. Some may see in their decisions something extraordinary. Indeed, they have made heroic choices. But they are not alone. Parents make similar sacrifices.

Every day you rise at dawn to go to work to support your family, you are self-giving. Every time you do without something you want so that your children can have what they need, you are just like Chris and Bill. Think about it: after years of loving, educating, encouraging, nurturing and sacrificing for your child, what's your ultimate purpose? To let them go so that they can create a unique existence, independent of the very people who formed them, just as Bill and Chris live so that their people will know freedom as God's children. Detachment is never easy. But it's the way we choose to love others more fully than ourselves. It's a power each of us has for making God's world a better place.

Questions for Reflection

● Is the comparison that Father Jim makes between missionary work and parenthood farfetched? What sacrifices have you made in serving your family?

The Past as Past

WEARING clerical clothing is a terrific magnet. People respond to our priestly uniforms in a variety of ways, but they certainly do react. In the best of circumstances, you get a kindly nod of the head and a smile that says "Good to see you, Padre!" Then there are looks it's harder to categorize. Some people seem intrigued that anyone does what we do for a living. Some gaze at you as if you were more an object than a person. But, by far, the most interesting are those with a bone to pick. These folks would never call or write to complain, but with a priest right in front of them, they reason, "This is my chance to tell him what I think of them all!" They also seem to think that talking to one priest will get the message to every priest.

In one exchange, a woman waylaid me at an airport to ask if I knew her town's priest, Father Paul. I asked her the priest's last name. She wasn't sure. Then I asked her where her home-town was located. She told me it was in northern Minnesota. I explained that I come from New York and don't know many priests from Minnesota. The woman looked a little puzzled. "I thought that you all knew each other," she admitted.

At a recent wedding reception, a man came up to tell me that while he was baptized a Catholic Christian, he "hasn't seen the inside of a church for almost forty years." Presuming he wanted to tell me his story, I asked, "How come?" Seems that when he was about twenty years old, he heard a priest preach a sermon he didn't like. The priest was his pastor and apparently suggested that people should donate a particular percentage of their income to the church. Nothing new about this; most folks recognize "tithing" as a type of responsible stewardship. But for this disgruntled listener, it was too much. He told me, "You know, I really resented that guy telling me how much I should put in the basket. That's my decision, Father, not his!"

He's certainly right about that. Each person must decide for himself or herself what is an affordable amount to share with our faith community. But for me, a larger question remained. So I asked it.

"You mean that you stayed away from praying with your faith community, reflecting with them over the sacred scriptures and receiving the sacraments for forty years because of one priest and a message you didn't like?" The man nodded. "Well," I concluded, "that seems like a very dear price to pay."

That man is not unique. I have met many people who've left their home faith communities because of past slights or misunderstandings. Yes, hurt is a difficult thing to handle. But isn't working out our differences equally vital? Isn't seeing our religion as bigger than the relationship we have with a single person equally important?

I have met a few priests, who, from my viewpoint, just didn't measure up, but they never cost me my beliefs. Probably because I recognized them as members of a church, not the whole community. Can you imagine how few homes would be intact if every time people fought or disagreed someone walked out? Families, friendships and marriages endure because we acknowledge differences, express disappointments, try to heal wounds, and then move on. Human beings don't have perfect relationships. But part of the glory of all faiths is the power to forgive, the grace to be reconciled.

The man I told you about happened to be a Catholic, but the same story could be told in any religious community. I can't help but hope that he—and those like him—will look again at the great good they miss when they use the mistakes of the past as an excuse for not celebrating a spiritual present. They might be surprised by all the good that's been done these past forty years. What a shame if they miss the next forty!

Questions for Reflection

- Despite the disappointments and hurts you've encountered because of a priest, what makes it possible for you to stay in the Church?

- How do you help someone who has left the Church because of a real or imagined problem?

No Accidents, No Mistakes

SOME people, you just remember. It's not just their looks or intelligence. It's something in their presence, their very essence. That was my reaction when I first heard Kay C. James speak. A beautiful, charming, self-possessed, articulate woman, she commands your attention by the sureness of her convictions. Kay James has held a number of major positions with the government and with charitable organizations. She was an executive with the Washington, D.C.-based One-on-One Foundation, and also served as President George Bush's Assistant Secretary for Public Affairs in the U.S. Department of Health and Human Services.

And some folks would suggest that gifted and accomplished person should never have been born.

Let me set the context. Among her many educational efforts, Kay James has also argued for the right of children to be born. As an African-American, she is keenly aware that few are targeted for abortion more frequently than poor black Americans. Following one presentation, Kay James was confronted by a woman who identified herself as a counselor at an abortion center. Her attack on James was deeply personal, suggesting that because Kay James dressed well and enjoyed a privileged lifestyle, she was in no position to advise the poor on their choice for abortion. The critic said: "Mrs. James, you don't know what you're talking about. You are obviously so middle-class that you can't relate to the needs of the poor. You don't understand why a poor woman would need abortion services to improve the quality of her life."

Now, Kay James is no fool. So she responded to the criticism with a question: "Tell me how would you counsel a woman who comes to you in tears and says, 'I'm pregnant and I don't know what I'm going to do. I already have four children. My husband is suffering from alcoholism and he physically abuses the children and me. He can't hold a job, and I don't know how I'm going to put food on the table.' "

The abortion counselor had a ready answer. "The most loving thing that woman could do would be to have an abortion. What loving mother would bring a child into the world under those circumstances? What quality of life could that child be expected to have?"

And then Kay James lowered the boom. "I have a vested interest in how you would counsel that woman, because that woman was my mother. And that fifth child she carried was me. And in case there is any doubt in your mind, the quality of my life is very, very good. My husband Charles and I have three children and have adopted a fourth. I was born into a family struggling against poverty and alcoholism, but I am an example of what the power of Jesus Christ can do in the life of a believer."

Many people in our society see children as a personal choice, or as an accident of timing, or as a mistake in planning. Kay James thinks differently. She knows that there never has been and never will be a child conceived who is a "mistake" or an "accident" in the mind of God. Others believe that only when conditions are close to "perfect" should we dare to let a child be born. But as Kay James's life indicates, sometimes the most imperfect of situations produce abundant blessings.

When Kay James was only seven weeks old in her burdened mother's womb, she had a unique and distinct set of fingerprints. No one in the world could match them. Because that's how we're made: individual, precious. And each of us has a purpose which is uniquely our own.

Kay James's mother knew that. The world is richer for her choice to give life a chance.

Question for Reflection

● Given testimonies like this, why do so many people still support abortion rights?

Letting Go

THE telephone message said it all: "Steven has no chance of recovery. The end is coming soon. Please come to bless and anoint our son." Steven was thirty years old and a lifetime parishioner, the youngest of several children in a close-knit family. From birth, Steven has battled cystic fibrosis. His life was in many ways a miracle. At the time of his diagnosis, in infancy, he was not expected to make it past five years of age. Owing to advances in medicine that was later amended to age fifteen. Then maybe twenty. His survival to see his thirtieth birthday had been a reason to rejoice. To get to that age wasn't easy, and included a lung transplant along the way.

On this night, his lungs and kidneys had finally failed. All that was left was the droning sound of the respirator, doing the breathing that Steven could no longer do for himself. He was deep in a coma, and there was no chance that he would return. Left to his own devices he would have already left us. His body remained alive because of machines. That's what I walked into at ten o'clock one night. And into the maelstrom of an animated family discussion. Steven's mother, convinced that mechanical life was not life at all. His father was equally convinced that he did not want to turn the machine off and end his son's earthly life. Both are great people who loved the son they had nurtured for so long. Both are people of hope, who saw that for the first time in Steven's earthly journey, hope was not temporal but heavenly.

Our discussion centered on the proper choice for Steven. The Catholic Church says that we are not morally obligated to use extraordinary means to sustain human life. A respirator fits into that category. And that view is most forcefully true when the "extraordinary means" will not result in recovery. Instead, we're encouraged to let nature take its course. Turning off the respirator is not "causing" him to die. In fact, keeping him on the machine prolongs a bodily life whose time has come. And does it to no advantage for Steven.

In time, his Dad saw the wisdom of letting Steven go home. And so, with parental consent, the machine was turned off. Steven slipped quietly and gently away.

The challenge faced by Steven's parents is no longer unique. People face this kind of decision every day. The best way to meet this challenge is through dialogue before we get to that point. Living wills that indicate who we are and what we believe can help. But making our intentions known to family and friends is the best assurance that our hopes for the end of our lives will be respected.

And, importantly, we need to see that life is of value, but not an absolute value. We come from God and our hoped-for eternity is with God. The end of life shouldn't be seen as a feared ending, but as a transition to a higher life and a higher level of love. Steven has moved past his body. Turning off a machine that could not give him true earthly life was the release that allowed Steven to experience the fullness of life in God.

For me it was a privilege: to share a family's pain is a grace; to participate in their important discussions about the love it takes to let go and let God; and to witness Steven's passage from this life to the next. The situation I've just described is something all of us face, one way or another. Don't read this and think it's about others. It's a wise and insightful family that talks about this issue today, so that tomorrow's outlook can be filled with fewer obstacles. Life is a great gift. Knowing how to leave can only enhance that precious gift.

Question for Reflection

- What steps have you taken or will you take to have your end-of-life decisions respected?

You Can Never Tell

SO I'm driving up Sixth Avenue in the heart of colorful Greenwich Village, when I spy a young man. His hair is glowing purple. He's pierced in various places. He's dressed in grungy leather and is walking to the music he hears from the CD ear plugs in both ears. I presume him to be part of an alternate culture I don't know and probably don't want to. When the light changes to red I stop the car, as chance would have it, in front of the local Catholic church. The young man lopes by. As I "tsk, tsk" in my head over the fallen state of young people, he does something I would never have expected. As he passes the church, the young man makes the sign of the cross. He probably thought no one saw him but the Guy upstairs. He was wrong. A nosy priest driving by, and possessed by the very human tendency to judge by appearances, was quickly put in his place.

Judgments are so easy to make. People seem, at times, so obvious. But we aren't really obvious at all. We have a depth of feelings, a well of personality and spiritual searching so often unseeable to the naked eye. And deciding we know someone because of their outward appearance is almost always folly. Years ago I worked in a poor parish with a large minority population. I remember, one snowy night, the panic of having my car die in one of the worst sections of that parish. Moments later three large, young African-American men approached me. My first response was fear. I was certain that they were up to no good. Imagine my surprise when one of them leaned into my window with the offer of help. And they were as good as their offer. One looked under the hood and tinkered with my troubled engine. Another ran up the block, returning in minutes with a can of dry gas, apparently just what I needed to get the car started again. Off I drove, grateful for the help, embarrassed by what had been in my heart, and hoping that my face didn't reveal my quick judgment.

About six months later, my parents, my sister and I traveled to London. We had just finished a terrific lunch and were heading over to the Portrait Museum around Trafalgar Square on the Underground, a subway system of great style. But what we didn't notice until it was too late was the young man hurtling down the escalator behind us. He rushed quickly past, but not before reaching into my sister's open bag and lifting her wallet. By the time she realized what had happened, he was out of reach. We wouldn't have feared him or even given him a second look. After all, he looked a lot like us.

I learned a good deal about appearances that year. I came to see that so many of our unfounded fears about others are based on useless generalizations. I'm less inclined to evaluate or judge based on skin color, style of dress, cut of the hair or the differences in our ethnic background. At least I thought I was better at this kind of evaluation. Then I drove up Sixth Avenue, saw that kid and slipped into some judgments about his style and type. With a single gesture, the making of the sign of the cross, I got the kick in the pants I deserved. I had no more business deciding I knew the kind of person he was than he would have if my Roman collar inclined him to write me off as just one more boring old priest. Giving people a chance to be who they truly are, without prejudice, isn't easy.

It takes a daily dose of tolerance, understanding and allowing each person to speak for himself or herself. Not an easy job, but one we must undertake if the phrase "do unto others as you would have them do unto you" is to have any meaning at all.

Question for Reflection

● What have you learned from misjudging someone or from being misjudged yourself?

Reading: A Lost Art

A FRIEND of mine with a solid background in the Church communications field recently took a job in a Catholic high school where, among other things, she's teaching an elective course in journalism.

On the first day of school, she asked students in that class for a show of hands: How many of you read a newspaper every day?

Nothing. Zilch.

After a long silence, one student made an effort to be helpful. "If my mother leaves the paper open on the breakfast table, I look at the front page." Another, clearly looking for a lifeline, posed a question: "Does the horoscope count?"

Welcome to the 21st Century. Reading is rapidly becoming one of the lost arts, and all too often whatever reading is being done is reading in all in the wrong places. There's evidence of that in the growth of the teen magazine field, where the emphasis is on pop culture, keeping up with fashion trends, even advice on sexual matters.

It used to be that television took the blame for the decline in serious reading among the young, and there's more than a grain of truth in that. In recent years it's the computer which has become the culprit, again with good reason. Anyone with young children or grandchildren around knows how quickly they develop computer skills, but that doesn't always mean that reading skills grow at the same time.

E-mailing and instant messaging have spawned a language all their own, in fact, with abbreviated words and phonetic spelling (in the interest, supposedly, of saving time and display space) substituting for proper English usage. There's even a "text message version" of the Bible (published by Westminster John Knox Press) in which, for example, the stately King James translation of Ecclesiastes: "A time to keep, and a time to cast away; a time to rend, and a time to sew; a time to keep silence, and a time to speak," is reduced to: "2keep & 2chuck; 2shut it & 2talk." If this is progress, let me off!

Good reading is never out of style. Almost 400 years ago, William Walker wrote: "Learn to read slow; all other graces will follow in their proper places." In our own time, American author Mason Cooley observed that reading "gives us some-place to go when we have to stay where we are."

I'm happy to say that the Christopher Awards recognize the importance of quality literature by spotlighting important books and authors every year. It's an honor to have as a member of the judging panel Charles Scribner III, of the well-known publishing family, whose father Charles Scribner, Jr., once noted: "Reading is a means of thinking with another person's mind; it forces you to stretch your own."

I don't know whether these thoughts will console my friend with her high-school classroom full of non-readers (aspiring jour-nalist non-readers, at that!), but that situation might already have been corrected. Even before the semester started, she had made arrangements to take part in a national publication's "newspaper in the classroom" program, so by now these budding writers should be reading away. Newspapers might not be anyone's idea of classic literature, of course, but they do have a way of spurring good reading habits in young people—not to mention a lively interest in what's going on in the world around them.

And I don't know whether the student who wanted to know, "Does the horoscope count?" ever got a reply. I think that I'd be inclined to answer, "Maybe—just maybe—it's a start."

Questions for Reflection

● Have you sacrificed reading time to the TV and computer? Is it worth regaining?

Time on Your Hands

SO, how are you spending all that leisure time you've got on your hands?

If your mouth just fell open or if the thought flitted through your head that this column must be meant for somebody else, give me a minute. I know that you're busy. You have your job—you know, the one that lets you afford a place to live, put food on the table, and all the rest—work around the house, shopping and other errands. Don't forget getting the children to school and, of course, their other activities, your obligations to parents, church, and the additional commitments you've taken on. Add in efforts at "quality time" with family and friends. And who would begrudge you an occasional night on the town—or on your couch? No doubt, you can come up with an even longer list of things you have to do.

No argument from me that you are busy. But I would like to point out that the English word leisure comes from the Latin for "to be permitted." I want to encourage you to give yourself permission to spend your time as carefully—yet generously—as you do your money.

OK, I'm making some assumptions here. But most people are very concerned, if not actually worried, about finances these days. Layoffs, cutbacks, recession are some of the troubling factors on everybody's minds as they stretch dollars and budgets. The amazing thing is that there has never been a time when people have been as determined to help others in need. And folks are in need. Every town and every country has men, women and children lacking the most basic necessities. And, at the same time, every neighborhood still tries to meet social, educational and cultural demands that make life a little more human, a little more meaningful. Here are a couple of people who have decided to take time to do good:

• Jean Zecha has grandchildren to care for, but makes time to volunteer at a soup kitchen once a month. She says, "I don't feel that I'm especially talented or outgoing, but I can give of myself—and that is what faith is all about, sharing of one's time and self."

• James O'Neill attends town meetings, writes letters and makes phone calls to let politicians know his views. "Why?" he asks. "I believe it is a part of living out my faith and showing concern for the poor and voiceless."

"I want to do something" has become a common expression of the desire to reach out to others, to give of one's self. I won't pretend that carving time out of your schedule for what is, essentially, service to others will be easy, but I guarantee it will be worth it. Listen to the words of two people who are celebrated for their service to humanity:

The only ones among you who will be really happy are those who have sought and found how to serve.   —Albert Schweitzer

Not everybody could be famous but everybody can be great because greatness is determined by service.

—Martin Luther King, Jr.

Both happy and great—what more could anyone ask? Offer your self, your compassion, your time and you will gain as immeasurably as you give.

Question for Reflection

•   Are you satisfied with the time you give to others who are in need? What more can you offer?

"Right on Time" with Grace and Prayer

WHEN you're a kid, the opportunity of going away for something is very alluring. Whether it's to a camp or to a conference, it's "away" and that makes it sound like an adventure. I remember one such experience that actually changed some of my thinking.

Intrigued by an essay-writing contest, I'd submitted a high school student's view of why communism could in no way match the values of democracy. I not only won the contest, but was awarded the prize of a trip to our nation's capital. We'd been there as a family, but this was different. Here I'd be with several hundred others from around the country. And I'd be their special guest, one of the few teens in attendance.

The conference focused on the dangers of communism. There was a lineup of noteworthy people who spoke, including the dynamic Governor of California, Ronald Reagan. Filled with youthful enthusiasm, I returned home convinced that only far-reaching political, military, economic and social efforts, such as those discussed at the conference, could defeat a totalitarian threat.

Meanwhile, at church, my parish community as well as thousands like it continued a longstanding tradition of regularly praying for the conversion of Russia. I would join those around me in the special prayers said at the end of Mass. But I must admit that, in my heart, I doubted they'd do very much good. After all, I reasoned, communism was a powerful force for evil. It wasn't going to be defeated by words uttered in a half-empty church. I could not have known how thoroughly wrong I was back then. I know it better now.

Communism fell in eastern Europe not because the United States of America and other democracies had more guns, more bombs or more political skills. Our nuclear arsenal was not the victor. Our economic superpower status didn't clinch the deal. No, the real end came because of the transformation of hearts and minds, in particular, the heart and mind of Mikhail Gorbachev.

Leader of the USSR in the late 1980's and early 1990's, he's been asked in interviews time and again to explain what caused him to finally determine that the communist system was untenable. Nowhere does he suggest that weapons or earthly powers changed his mind. Certainly, he realized that the collective economic system was fatally flawed. He became a champion of democratic socialism, acknowledging the universal hunger for freedom and the desire of men and women to articulate their personal values. A sense of something "bigger than himself" compelled him to urge the twin goals of *glasnost* (openness) and *perestroika* (reform).

That something, I now believe, was the power of prayer. For so many years, in quiet churches throughout the world, millions had petitioned the Almighty for the grace of freedom. And that power, the force of sincere prayer, is the greatest catalyst in the world. I had forgotten something that had been said at that long ago conference, as well as in all those churches around the world where people prayed so steadfastly: in the long-run, no evil can prevail in the face of God's grace. And that grace was nurtured by the petitions of so many who dared to dream of a world of freedom.

A Gospel song that teaches: "He may not be there when you want Him, but the Lord, He's always right on time." In His time and way, God brings all good to fruition. Through prayer, as well as positive action, it is our job to be ready for Him.

Question for Reflection

● Do you believe that our actions have something to do with "God's perfect timing"?

Meeting Samantha Again

WHEN you're a priest in a large church, you know people by sight. But truth is, you don't always get to know everyone's name. In a parish like mine, with over four thousand families, you're fortunate to learn a few hundred first names. Some people understand this; others don't. They'll come up to you and very aggressively ask, "Do you know my name, Father?" I used to say, "Sure," and try to change the topic. But too often they'd call me on it. So now I just tell the truth: "No, I know your face, but your name escapes me." Some get a little miffed. "But you did my sister's wedding three years ago," said one. "That," I responded, "was three hundred weddings ago." A similar moment happened recently, but I was happy for the confrontation.

An attractive young woman approached me after Mass. She waited until all the other folks had left before asking, "Do you know who I am?" I didn't. So I asked, "Have we met before?" "Well, yes, in a very unusual way." Now she had my curiosity aroused. "Tell me where and when," I asked. "My name is Samantha. I'm eighteen. You actually knew my mother back when she was pregnant with me. So that's when we met, it just wasn't face to face."

I asked her to tell me more. "My mother raised me alone. She had very little financial or emotional support. Her parents didn't like my biological father. He apparently left the scene once Mom became pregnant. So here she was, just nineteen at the time – pregnant, alone, poor and scared."

How, I wondered, did I fit into this story? Samantha continued: "I recently asked my mother why she didn't get an abortion. She said she almost did. But she happened upon a priest who gave a talk on the beauty of human life, and the need to protect it. You. She looked for you after Mass and you two talked. Just like we're talking now. My Mom says she expected you to get angry at her when she said that she was pregnant and considering an abortion. But you didn't. You just hugged her and offered to help her to have me. She said that when she cried with fear about raising a child alone, your eyes filled up too."

I asked Samantha to tell me more. "My Mom says you two talked for over an hour. And then, as Mom said she needed time to think about her options, you offered her a blessing and prayed for me too. Mom says that blessing made her realize that there really were two of us, Mom and me. I stopped being a problem and became a someone to her for the first time. I stopped being a crisis and became her child."

I wish I could say that I knew or remembered the encounter, but I don't. I wish I could say that I knew just the right words to say back then, but I didn't. Like many times in my life as a priest, I think God just used me as His instrument, and it's foolish to claim credit for saying the good stuff!

Samantha concluded, "When I heard that story I had to find out where you worked. I just needed to tell you that I'm grateful that you and my Mom met when you did. She needed someone to listen, someone to care. She needed not to be condemned for what she was thinking of doing but to be loved enough to see the positive possibilities. You did that and I think that's why I got to be born. So, listen, when you're tired or having a bad day or when all the scandal stuff in the Church gets you down, please don't forget that sometimes your life has more meaning than you know. Thanks for being there for my Mom. Thanks for being there for me."

Questions for Reflection

- Reflect and share about a time when someone's listening helped you through a crisis.
- Recall a time when you were there for someone else.

Part V

Paying It Forward

In His Hands

KIM Kim Dae Jung has been tested all his life. A citizen of South Korea, he came early in life to see the value of freedom, and committed himself to the principles which underlie democracy. That might not be a difficult vocation were he born in a democratic country. But he wasn't. He was raised in a nation which had a continuous line of military dictatorships. And the people who led his nation decided early on that he should be silenced. Over the years, he endured prison, house arrest, exile and constant surveillance.

Kim Dae Jung never let these intimidations keep him quiet. Instead, he spoke out however and wherever he could. So vexing was this free-thinking and free-speaking individual that the government decided he needed to be taught a final lesson. Writes Jung: "In August of 1973, while exiled in Japan, I was kidnapped from my hotel room in Tokyo by intelligence agents of the then military government of South Korea. The agents took me to their boat at anchor along the seashore. They tied me up, blinded me and stuffed my mouth." These agents were about to kill this troublesome dissident and bring his cry for freedom to a permanent end.

Jung, a Catholic Christian, decided that his only choice was surrender. No, not to the pressures of his captors. But surrender to the will of God. He recalled the valuable lessons from holy men and women of faith who put aside their fears and their anxieties. They let go. They let God be the master of their lives. Jung describes what happened next: "Just when they were about to throw me overboard, Jesus Christ appeared before me with such clarity. I clung to Him, and begged Him to save me. At that very moment, rescuers appeared and won my release."

Kim Dae Jung is no ordinary freedom fighter, but one of many tireless voices who refused to be silent. After years of dictatorships, the popular will for freedom finally prevailed and South Korea embraced democracy. Several years ago, Kim Dae Jung was elected President of South Korea.

Seeking to be a reconciler for all the people of the Korean peninsula, he boldly proposed to visit the forbidden nation of North Korea. He went with no expectations beyond a desire for dialogue and an end to the hostilities which have separated North and South for a half century. It was daring. And it bore fruit. The relationship between the Koreas has softened. Families kept apart for decades by the demilitarized zone are able to see each other at last.

Kim Dae Jung's devotion to the cause of justice and belief that one life can make a difference has been rewarded. In 2001 he received the Nobel Peace Prize. In his remarks at Oslo, Jung summed up his philosophy of hope: "In 1980, I was sentenced to death by the military regime. For six months, in prison, I awaited my execution day. Often I shuddered with fear of death. But I would find calm in the historical fact that justice ultimately prevails. I knew that in all ages, in all places, he who lives a righteous life dedicated to his people and humanity may not be victorious, may meet a gruesome end in his lifetime, but will be triumphant and honored in history. He who wins by injustice may dominate the present day, but history will always judge him to be a shameful loser. There can be no exception."

Kim Dae Jung did not, thank God, need to wait for history to vindicate him. In his lifetime, he has seen the result of persistence, dedication, courage and conviction. Just one person with a dream, but a dream with the fire of justice is, in the end, unstoppable.

Question for Reflection

● What inspires you most about Kim Dae Jung's philosophy of hope?

Last Place Lessons

THEY set new records at the 2001 New York Marathon. Tesfaye Jifar of Ethiopia beat the existing men's record by 18 seconds with his time of 2 hours 7 minutes 43 seconds. It was his first marathon win ever. Margaret Okayo of Kenya came in at 2 hours 24 minutes 21 seconds for a new women's course record. Later she said that for the whole run, "I was thinking about finishing the race and doing my best."

That's probably true of the other 30,000 runners who gather on the first Sunday in November to take on each other and themselves. It was certainly true for Zoe Koplowitz, who took part in her fourteenth straight New York Marathon. For the fourteenth time, she came in last.

Zoe Koplowitz did not cross the finish line until Monday morning. It always takes her more than 24 hours to cover the 26.2-mile race because she has multiple sclerosis and needs two crutches to go the distance.

The 53-year-old has had MS for more than twenty years, but it was not until she nearly died that she decided to change her life. After choking on a vitamin pill and being saved by the Heimlich maneuver, Ms. Koplowitz "decided I needed to do the most outrageous thing I could imagine."

What could be more outrageous for someone with her major health problems (she also has diabetes) than entering a marathon? With the help of the Achilles Track Club, an organization for runners with disabilities, she trained and got through the first marathon, ultimately crossing a deserted finish line. But in the years since, the determined woman admits she has "become a symbol of endurance" for thousands.

Learning of her achievement, the Multiple Sclerosis Society asked her to be the ambassador for its annual fundraising walk. She has also participated in the Boston and London marathons. Ms. Koplowitz has become a popular motivational speaker and the author of a book, *Winning Spirit: Life Lessons Learned in Last Place.* Over and over, she has been thanked by people with disabilities and all who are astounded by her persistence for reminding them that, however difficult, life is worth living.

Nobody needs to be told these days that life can be painful. Everyone who ran or watched the New York Marathon knows it. Anyone who looks at the nightly news knows about life's uncertainty and anguish. But for most of us, our greatest challenges will never come from the skies or the mail. It will come from within, from our own bodies and minds and souls. Either way, it helps to see the "everyday heroes" who do what they have to do to achieve their goals—or at least give it their very best effort.

That's why Zoe Koplowitz's annual 26.2-mile slow, determined walk buoys up so many. "It's my mission to help people reinvent the way they think about 'winning,' " she says. "I believe people run marathons every day of their lives in one way or another, and we need to remember to give ourselves the finishers' medals we deserve."

She also says, "What I do is a metaphor for life, just like the marathon itself. It means you get somewhere by putting one foot after another."

One foot in front of another is the only way anyone gets anywhere.

Question for Reflection

● Who would you nominate for a Finisher's Medal?

Great Guests, All

FATHER James Keller, founder of The Christophers, was a visionary who determined to use the media—print, radio and television—to spread his message: each one of us can make a difference for the better and each of us uniquely matters. These ideas resonated strongly in the minds and hearts of countless people.

Starting in 1952, Father Keller used television in a particularly powerful way. Through interviews with interesting and accomplished persons, famous and less so, he encouraged viewers to see that each life counts, that none of us is an accident or a mistake, that as long as we live, we possess the possibility of improving the world. Since 2002 marked fifty years of Christopher television, we decided to go back to Hollywood, a place Father Keller visited often, to produce new *Christopher Closeup* programs.

Our guests were twelve people we've come to admire and appreciate through the years. Let me tell you some of the outstanding stories they had to tell.

Comedian and author Dom DeLuise is one of the funniest people alive. He spoke of the hope laughter brings. Dom believes that you don't have to do amazing things for people in need, that small things matter more. The ability to draw laughter or a smile can be a great gift to those who are sad or disheartened. His words reminded me of Mother Teresa's famous lesson: "Peace begins with a smile." In so many ways, joyous Dom DeLuise is a true peacemaker.

Lou Ferrigno, known to most as *The Incredible Hulk*, was a poignant and inspiring guest. He told us about losing most of his hearing as a child. For years, his disability made him feel embarrassed and ashamed. But his parents, a gentle mother and a strong-willed father, would not allow Lou to give in to emotional paralysis. Instead, they sent young Lou to a school that would strengthen and empower him. Lou came to know, as he told us, "that every one of us is disabled or handicapped in one way or another. For some that disability is physical. For others emotional. But no disability needs to make us give up on living life fully." Now starring in the TV series *The King of Queens*, he lives that lesson each day.

Chrystee Pharris is a beautiful young African-American actress. Formerly on the inspiring WBTV series *7th Heaven*, she now stars in the NBC series *Passions*. But it almost didn't happen. Early in her career, Chrystee was offered a major movie role at a time she badly needed employment. This would be her big break. Finally she'd be able to pay her rent! Then she read the script. As a person of faith and morals, Chrystee was crestfallen. The part called for nudity. Believing that was wrong, she decided not to accept this part. Her agent warned her that a chance like this might not come again. In tearful prayers, Chrystee Pharris promised the Lord that she'd hold fast to her promise. No part was worth her dignity.

Two days later, another script appeared at Chrystee's doorstep. It was an equally important opportunity and she would not need to compromise her beliefs and values. Chrystee had been true to her God. She felt God was faithful to her as well.

Whatever our role in life, we are all asked to be faithful to God and to our best selves.

Question for Reflection

- Putting false humility aside, can you see how being faithful to God can improve the world?

More Guests to Meet

WHEN our producers told me that one of our guests for our *Christopher Closeup* series when we made a recent visit to Hollywood would be the game show host Monty Hall, I was happy and intrigued. I'd always loved his wonderful, spirited work on *Let's Make A Deal*, but wondered just how he reflected the Christopher spirit. I didn't have to look far.

He told us the wonderful story of his maternal grandfather who left the Ukraine in 1901 with virtually nothing. In fact, they were so poor that his wife and children had to be left behind for several years. When Monty's grandfather arrived in Canada, he was surprised and delighted when someone he didn't know offered him room and board until he could get settled. That offer of charity had a profound impact on this new immigrant. It led to the development of a sense of responsibility throughout his family to help those in need. This was a mandate Monty Hall took very seriously indeed.

Now 78 years old, Monty Hall has raised over a billion dollars for charity. More to the point, the use of his fame to assist the needy has deeply inspired others. Monty tells the story of a call he received from actor Steve Guttenberg. This successful young actor (also a *Christopher Closeup* guest) had reached a point where he knew that he had to give something back for all the blessings he'd received. So he called Monty Hall and told him: "I want to get into doing more for charity and, around Hollywood, everyone agrees that you're the standard for getting involved and doing good for others. How can I get involved?"

Steve Guttenberg now directs charities that help to restore eyesight to those who might otherwise have no hope. He also founded Guttenhouse, a home for homeless teens.

Yet another impressive guest was broadcast legend Art Linkletter. Host to three of television's most successful shows, he has always enjoyed a special insight into the human soul. His book and TV series *Kids Say the Darndest Things* (now under the care of comedian Bill Cosby) continues to touch and amuse. Art addressed his belief that the family is perhaps God's greatest gift to us. He spoke lovingly of his wife Lois. Married now for sixty-six years, he credits her with keeping him honest, humble and strong. He shared the remembrance of his daughter's drug-related suicide. Without God, his family and, especially, his beloved Lois, it would have been simply too much. Art Linkletter reminded us to acknowledge and treasure our family members.

I think the founder, Father James Keller, would have enjoyed meeting these talented men. And I believe he would be delighted that fifty years after the start of Christopher television, we still celebrate the many ways people in all walks of life continue to make a positive difference for our world.

Question for Reflection

● Who has been a Monty Hall—a model for getting involved and doing good for others—in your life?

Saints Alive! And Well, Too

IF your first encounter with saints came from looking at stained glass windows in church, you are not alone. I suspect that lots of youngsters whose parents told them to stop fidgeting and pay attention, noticed those colorful images of people in long gowns with their heads surrounded by halos.

Unfortunately, too many of us got the impression that the saints were all long ago and far away. Persons who, if not exactly myths or legends, were not real people. They weren't just holy, they were perfect. And, while we learned differently over the years, some of our original perceptions probably stuck. So, of course, we can't quite believe that there are saints alive and well right now, or that they might be closer to us than we think.

With due deference to the folks canonized by the Catholic Church, all of God's faithful people are called to holiness. No religion has a monopoly. Saints start out simply by being flesh and blood people who take the word of God to heart. They generally live ordinary lives in extraordinary ways: They pray, they love and they serve. Like all of us they are prone to doubt, discouragement, fear and anger. But because they know, really know deep in their souls that God is with them, they never give up.

Here's one good description I came across of what makes a saint a saint:

They are cheerful when it is difficult to be cheerful.

They are patient when it is difficult to be patient.

They push on when they want to stand still.

They keep silent when they want to talk.

They are agreeable when they want to be disagreeable.

That is all. It is quite simple, and always will be.

Maybe that sounds a little more like people you know. Those open to God's grace strive to promote His justice, peace and mercy. They love and forgive, they pray and act. What they are not—is perfect.

In the introduction to his fine book, *All Saints: Daily Reflections on Saints, Prophets, and Witnesses for Our Time*, Robert Ellsberg writes: "No, the saints are not perfect humans. But in their own individual fashion they became authentic human beings, endowed with the capacity to awaken that vocation in others. Dorothy Day . . . did not like to be called a saint: 'When they call you a saint, basically it means you are not to be taken seriously.' This book offers a different argument: that to call someone a saint means that his or her life should be taken with the utmost seriousness. It is proof that the gospel can be lived."

Proof, indeed.

A fellow priest once asked a youngster, "What do you think a saint is?" Remembering the figures in the stained glass windows at church, the child answered, "A saint is someone the light shines through."

On the feast of All Saints, it's worth considering that before God's holy people become stained glass images, they are men and women who have to get up every morning, face themselves in the mirror and know that they will give life the very best they can . . . and with God's help the light will shine through.

Questions for Reflection

● Trying on Father Jim's description of what makes a saint a saint, where do you measure up? Where do you need to grow?

Beginning Again

YOU'D know his face right away. He's one of those actors who always seem to be working. That's unusual in a profession where most members of the actors' union are unemployed. Television watchers know him best as Dr. David Hayward, the evil, menacing physician on the long-running soap opera *All My Children*. His name is Vincent Irizarry, and before his current success he was a regular on *Guiding Light*, a role that earned him an Emmy nomination. He's had a number of TV and film roles including an abusive husband opposite Sissy Spacek in *Marie—A True Story* and with Clint Eastwood in *Heartbreak Ridge*.

All of this represents the fulfillment of a quest that started in Vincent's youth. At the age of eleven, he got interested in photography. He became a classically trained pianist, and while attending college to study music, discovered his gift for acting. By any standard, Vincent Irizarry is an American success story.

In the midst of his successful career, Vincent also fell in love, married and became the father of a beautiful daughter named Siena. Most folks would say he had it all: money, recognition, a great wife and child. Vincent knew differently. As a recent guest on the television series *Christopher Closeup*, he explained how superficial his life was. All he had was rooted in the values of this world and not the next. He lacked a spiritual foundation, and when storms hit (as they inevitably do for everyone), he ran adrift. Three years into the marriage, it came apart. That reality hit Vincent hard. He'd been raised in a family where marriage was forever. His parents made it through the challenges of raising six children and all the ups and downs that come with family life. It was incomprehensible to Vincent that he couldn't have the same stable life for his new family. The divorce left him depressed and hurting. He developed a jaded sense of his future, convinced that permanent happiness was an illusion. Happily, he got a second chance.

Many people enter into second marriages. But Vincent decided to do it differently. He recognized that in his first attempt at marriage and family living, he'd let the things society says are important rule his life and lifestyle. No more. He knew he needed a better anchor than that. And, for him, that anchor was the Lord and the Scriptures. Vincent joined a prayer group. Worship and prayer became as much a part of his life as eating and sleeping. God was no longer an "add on" to his life, but its central truth. In time he came to see that fame and fortune are not, in and of themselves, evil. Everything depends on what you do with it.

As an example, Vincent mentioned that some of his fans wanted to create a club and Web site. The newly focused actor thought that idea was shallow and pointless, until he came to see that it didn't have to be about him. His fans' energy could be used to raise money for charities. So he green-lighted the creation of "Friends of Vincent Irizarry" to assist a non-profit organization called "Hope for New York." Working to help homeless people, AIDS patients and children in need who could benefit from tutoring, Vincent put his fame to good use.

He credits the development of his newfound generosity to a focus on faith. About embracing Christianity, Irizarry says: "It's the most glorious and significant thing to happen in my life." Vincent admits that he wasn't such a likable guy in those "successful" early years. He doubts he was much loved by people, and he doesn't blame them. But, realizing that when you're talking about God there are always second chances, he changed.

God's mercy is unconditional and He's always on your side. You just have to be willing to accept that always waiting, always loving embrace.

Question for Reflection

● How did God's giving you a second, third, fourth chance change you?

Finally at Peace

HAVING the legendary actor Carroll O'Connor as a guest on *Christopher Closeup* was a genuine thrill. Like most adult Americans, I grew up with his beloved if irascible incarnation of Archie Bunker. Carroll O'Connor was a terribly gifted man who managed to teach us both right and wrong through the opinionated blue-collar Archie. We could laugh at him, but we also understood that the limits of his tolerance were sometimes a mirror of our own prejudices and limitations. Years later Carroll gave us another challenging portrayal in the television drama, *In The Heat of the Night*. In their unique and powerful ways, both his comedy and drama series taught us about the need to live the Golden Rule. It's a lesson Carroll O'Connor tried to live throughout his life. And it pained him when all his efforts came up short.

I remember asking Carroll if he felt that his programs had advanced the cause of racial harmony in the twenty-five years since he first came to prominence. With an expression etched with sadness, he said that he doubted it. "After *All In The Family* and *In the Heat of the Night*, we're still dragging black men to their deaths in places like Jasper, Texas. So how far have we really come, Father Jim?"

But ever the optimist, Carroll said he had confidence that what we lack the ability to accomplish, would, through the grace of God, be made right one day. That outlook especially reflected his attitude toward the tragic loss of his son. Hugh, the child adopted by Carroll and his beloved wife, Nancy, was the apple of his eye. Brought back from Italy as an infant, he never lacked for the dedicated love of his parents. But all the love in the world can't always thwart the path of drug addiction. For years, Hugh wrestled with this demon. And his parents wrestled along with him. If they could have willed him to sobriety, they would have. If they could have offered their lives in place of his, they would have. But it was not to be. Driven to despair, Hugh took his own life. In a way, Carroll's heart died on the same day as his son's.

Oh, he did what he could to spread the message about resisting drugs. He did continue to love his widowed daughter-in-law and his grandson. He worked a bit. He went to Mass each week in the company of his wife of half a century, praying for peace. But, truth told, he also carried a sadness that would not be lifted. Friends say he aged significantly in the years following Hugh's death.

At our television interview, O'Connor spoke of Hugh with gentleness and a proud love. But he was struggling, still. You'd see it in the sorrowful tone, in the eyes that longed to see his son again.

Then, toward the end of our conversation, the topic turned to life beyond this life. I asked Carroll if he believed that our lives continue beyond the earthly journey. His answer was unequivocal: "Absolutely." Then I asked him if he thought that Hugh was alive and living in heaven. Again, the certainly: "Without a doubt." And with my final question, a gentle smile returned to his face. "Carroll," I asked, "do you expect to meet Hugh again in the hereafter?" I will always remember his twinkling eyes and the certainty with which he said, "Oh, yes."

Sadly, we have lost an actor of great talent and charm. Sadly, his family is without a husband, a father-in-law and a grandfather whom they adored. But I know of one place where there is surely great happiness. And that's in a place we call heaven, where a father and his son are joined in a loving and much longed for embrace. Rest in peace, dear Carroll, dear Archie, you have well earned your place in Paradise.

Questions for Reflection

- How can you help someone who loses a loved one to suicide?
- How sure are you—after taking their life—that they are living in heaven?

Doing Their Duty

THERE are many facts I know about my Dad. Born in 1920 to an Italian-American family, he worked his way through college. Following military service during World War II, he became a New York City police officer. He followed this with a stint as an NYPD detective, while attending law school at night. During those years, he also married my Mom and began a family. He retired in the 1980's and spends the best of his times now in her company and that of his grandchildren.

In the stories Dad tells about his life and career, he almost never details the years in which he served as a Marine captain in the Pacific theater. When urged, he gives short answers. I know, from the medals in a trunk I found in their garage, that he served with honor. But he never takes them out or mentions them. For baby-boomers like myself, something here is beyond understanding. I can't imagine fighting in a World War, being wounded, seeing good friends die in the name of freedom, and not talking about it.

One time I pressed him on this. "Dad, why don't you talk more about your experiences in the War? It had to be one of the most significant experiences imaginable, right?" He didn't deny it and went into great detail about boot camp, recalling the challenges and hardships faced by those green young men. Interesting, but again without focus on the war itself. So I asked, "What about the battlefields?" He was quiet. Finally, he told me of the battles and the sadness. But he also gave me insight into the essential silence of his generation.

"You see, Jim, what I did was not very special. We were all there. Everyone served and everyone was at risk. What I did was no better or worse than anyone else. We were all expected to do our duty. And most of us did. And the price was very high. So many died or were wounded. So many young men, eighteen and nineteen, paid the ultimate price. They never got to experience all the joys I have. Marrying your mother . . . having children . . . playing with my grandchildren . . . having a career I enjoyed. So what we did was good, but it doesn't require any special attention. In the end, we were the blessed ones. We got to come home."

My father isn't unique. These people heard the call of duty and responded with a generous spirit. They don't seem to have been paralyzed by the inclinations of those in my own generation and beyond. For countless numbers of us, demands on our time and energy have to have a purpose that will benefit us personally. The notion of doing something for the greater good, if you will never gain personally from that sacrifice, just isn't popular. And that's too bad. Because there is something noble about these folks, many passing away each day as they reach their seventies, eighties and beyond. People who gave without counting the cost. People who were willing to recognize that the offering of their own lives could one day lead to a better world. People like my Dad, self-effacing and self-giving. People who are or should be models and heroes for generations to come.

My parents dated before the war, but didn't marry until it was over. They decided, like many in that time, to put their personal commitment on hold. With the war's end, they finally walked down the aisle. My father remembers that great day as a combination of joy and sadness. Joy for himself, his wife and their families. But a sadness at the knowledge that too many friends would never take that walk.

The next time we look at the slightly stooped, aging people who are our parents and grandparents, we might say a silent prayer of thanksgiving. They embody the very meaning of selfless love, and we are all richer for their sacrifices.

Question for Reflection

● In addition to praying for your aging parents and grandparents, how can you acknowledge their selfless acts of love—even if they have died?

What Lola Wants

INTERVIEWING Lola Falana was not the experience I expected. This woman, after all, enjoyed the nickname "First Lady of Las Vegas" because she was a performer par excellence. As a co-star to Sammy Davis, Jr. on Broadway, a guest star on TV shows ranging from *Hullabaloo* to *Mad About You* and a regular on Ben Vereen's series, this was a woman who had it all. Blessed with stunning looks, a great ability to dance and sing and a winning personality, the standout actress had created in me a very specific set of expectations. None matched the woman I recently met through a different kind of television experience.

It seems that through all those years, Lola Falana knew something was missing. She defined herself as "an empty person with a strong sense that this is not what it's all about." So she did what we're all supposed to do when we feel lost: she prayed—prayed that God would show her a new direction, a path that might lead to wholeness and personal peace because all the money and fame weren't doing the job.

God responded, she says, in a curious and wonderful way. She came down with multiple sclerosis. And more strangely, perhaps, she ended up thanking God for this gift. Because for this "can do" person, MS changed everything. It freed her from the constraints of long-term contracts and obligations. It took her from the stage and left her with time for prayer, reflection and a search for meaning. Now, Lola feels she's found it.

The woman who once reveled in sequins and jewelry now looks very different. Her only jewelry now is a plain cross worn around her neck as a simple reminder of the faith which anchors her. Financially, things have also changed. Lola Falana once commanded up to $90,000 a week as an entertainer.

Now, she draws no salary. Instead, she spends her days on the road, visiting churches throughout the country as a lay evangelist. She tells people her story of conversion, of finding the true meaning in life. And what is that truth? In our interview, Lola Falana shared some of the insights she's discovered over the past few years.

Lola admitted that she now sees the harm in senseless vanity and the zillions of dollars we spend to make something more of ourselves than we're meant to. God made us beautiful, she says, as we are. All the jewelry, makeup, plastic surgery and fancy clothing can't improve on the essential beauty of our souls. In her quest for more and more financial success, Lola discovered another truth: all the money you make in no way guarantees happiness or peace. After a while, it's just money for money's sake.

And the blessings that came from her MS? Lola says she came to recognize that we are meant to be dependent on God, our Creator. In our human arrogance, we often presume to act as if we invented or created ourselves. Illness, she says, reminds us that we come from God and return to God. He is our starting point and our final destination. And illness can also make us more prayerful, compassionate, sensitive and more aware of our real purpose in our human journey. That purpose, Lola suggests, is to give and give and then give again. It is, simply put, to make the world a better place because we lived here.

Interviewing Lola Falana is jarring. You expect a dazzling stage beauty, but you find beauty of another kind: a very attractive woman whose allure is not superficial. Rather you are drawn to her generous heart, her peaceful smile, her ease of manner and her courageous convictions about our reliance on the wonder of God's goodness. Some might look at her and say she's given it all up. I'd say Lola's finally found it all.

Question for Reflection

● Lola seems to have chosen the best part of her illness, instead of feeling sorry for herself. What good has come out of an experience of loss in your life?

Connery Calling

FOR more than ten years, I've been involved with television production. As host and executive producer of a weekly interview program, it has been my job to find guests from all walks of life. People from the arts, professional sports and government service usually give interesting interviews. Plus, people recognize their faces and stop to watch.

Booking guests isn't as easy as you might think. Noted people want to know who watches the show, what the theme or direction of the program is, and what the advantage of appearing will be for them. And, frankly, you don't often get to talk to the talented folks you want as guests. Instead, you get their agents, managers or publicists and it's their job to determine the value of being on a program for their clients. These days everyone, from minor to major stars, seems to have this wall of protectors.

Oddly, those who don't have the greatest careers often have the most impregnable defense structure! For example, it took me twelve attempts to get through a myriad of handlers to contact a still-rising singer. Then he begged off twice. When he finally came on the show, he was difficult to deal with. Lighting, makeup and camera angles were not complimentary enough. And he couldn't sing for us, of course, unless the accompanying piano player was "top notch." This is someone just beginning to land a few favorable reviews!

There's no telling what fragile egos you run into in the entertainment world. Which brings me to a call I once received that delighted and surprised me. The Christophers present annual awards to outstanding books, television programs and movies. One film we honored for the year 2000 was *Finding Forrester*. It's a moving story about the mentoring relationship between an inner city African American teen and a reclusive Pulitzer Prize-winning novelist. One of the producers of this terrific film is its star, Sean Connery.

Now Sean Connery is a big star, an Academy Award winner, who has a success rate unmatched by most in the business. His international fame began with the James Bond films and continues forty years later without letup. He has, no doubt, agents, publicists, etc., so we wrote to him with little expectation of a positive answer. So imagine the look on my face as my assistant tells me "Mr. Connery's on the phone." Yeah, right. But, sure enough, on picking up the phone there's that very familiar Scottish brogue. "Hello, Jim, this is Sean Connery." I have friends who fake accents, but this was the real thing. Without fanfare, he gets to the point: "I'm so happy to receive the Christopher award. Thank you for that. But I'm stuck in Paris and can't make the awards ceremony in New York. Please give the people there my deep thanks. I appreciate this very much. Be well, lad. Bye now."

You're welcome, Sean.

It's a pleasure to find the normal and grateful where you might expect the puffed up. There is a huge difference between taking yourself seriously and taking your work seriously, between loving and respecting yourself and being completely absorbed with yourself. Whoever you are and whatever you do, a little humility and a lot of thankfulness are good for the soul—and they certainly make it easier for the folks around you to live with you!

Question for Reflection

● Who do you know who has done a good job of handling success?

Not Love, but Respect

GREGORY Allen Howard is a great man. A big man with a powerful presence, you can see that he must have been a formidable football player in his high school and college years. But his physical size only begins to express the scope of the man. For Greg Howard has a heart which has borne pain, yet risen to amazing heights by transforming the sadness into hope. He is a screenwriter, whose film *Remember the Titans*, addresses the suffering and sadness of racism.

Based on the integration of a Virginia High School football team in the late 1960's, the film demonstrates how, in the end, our humanity makes us more similar than we often admit. But writing this stunning script was not just an intellectual exercise for Greg Howard. As an African-American in a culture which still highlights the differences among people, Greg Howard knew, first-hand, the challenges of bigotry.

In an interview at The Christophers, Greg shared experiences of his life in California. He recounted how, time and time again, he was stopped while driving. He'd done nothing wrong, broken no laws, driven with care. But he was a black man driving through a white neighborhood and that was reason enough to be stopped, investigated, and (in his view) harassed just for being. His story is not unique. We hear it too often.

Now, Greg Howard had a choice, to close in and become embittered, or to be more positive. He chose the latter. He moved from Los Angeles back to Virginia, settling in Alexandria. He went there because he found it to be a truly integrated community. It's a place of balance and respect for the wonderful differences among peoples and races. There he wrote the script for *Remember the Titans*. This film, which stars Denzel Washington and Will Patton, is an unusual look at racism. There are no simply good or bad characters. Instead, it holds up a mirror of America, full of nuances and shades of gray. Two coaches, one black, one white, must work together to integrate their respective football teams into a unit. They accomplish the task from mutual positions of moral goodness. The movie does an outstanding job of showing well-intentioned people struggling to surmount differences and past misunderstandings.

At the heart of both Gregory Allen Howard's personal journey and the film's storyline is a simple message. It may be too much to expect that people of different colors and cultures can completely understand each other, as good as that would be. But we can travel the road to that goal through mutual respect. "You don't have to love me," Greg said, "but I demand your respect" based on our existence as children of God.

The movie (available on video and DVD) should be watched as a family. It will, inevitably, lead to the kinds of discussion that result in new perspectives and new hope.

Gregory Allen Howard, a winner of a Christopher Award for films, turned a negative reality into a positive good. *Remember the Titans* reveals a vision for a possible future built on mutual respect, understanding and, yes, love—if we choose to make it so.

See it and be moved by hope.

Question for Reflection

- During times of war and terrorist strikes, how can Gregory Howard's film help us to be more positive?

The Ultimate Search

WHEN the end-of-the-year commemorative magazines focused on the notable passing of people in 2001, most gave special attention to comic/TV host/author Steve Allen. They highlighted his role as the original host of *The Tonight Show,* among many impressive television firsts. By way of praise, commentary called him the forefather of the Johnny Carsons, the David Lettermans, the Jay Lenos and the Conan O'Briens. In fact, he was much, much more than that.

Shortly before Steve Allen died, I did an interview with him about faith, about values and about the life to come. His words now seem so ironic, spoken as he was so close to the end of his own earthly journey.

The most striking image I have of our time together was his humility. When words like "legend," "icon," or "important figure" were used, he'd dismiss them quickly. In his mind, important people were those who actually saved lives, people of heroism in action. He told me about an event he attended to reward people who unselfishly put themselves in harm's way. The dinner at which these folks were celebrated was built around Steve Allen as the celebrity host. Allen mentioned that he felt hopelessly insignificant next to the concrete ways these unknown individuals had made a difference for the good: they were firefighters, police officers and regular folks who bothered to get involved. Allen said that they, not TV personalities, were the people we should be bringing to our children and grandchildren's attention.

Beyond humility, I was also impressed with the important theological speculation Allen sorted through for many years. Raised in a Catholic home, he had felt estranged from the Church after a divorce from his first wife and a marriage to actress Jayne Meadows. This self-imposed exile also caused him to think long and hard about the existence of God and the afterlife. His conclusions, voiced so soon before his death, were telling.

He called himself a Christian agnostic. He'd often question the existence of God, but felt that if God exists, he most likely took the form of Jesus Christ. His belief in the reality of an afterlife was intimately tied to the injustices of this world. Steve Allen came to speculate that little in this life was just or fair. But heaven would correct all that. He said: "I can't find any justice in the world. That's why there has to be an afterlife. There's got to be justice in an afterlife, because there sure isn't any justice here."

Steve Allen, a man who made his public legacy primarily through television, acknowledged that some would view his criticism of the current state of TV entertainment as "biting the hand that feeds you." Nonetheless, he offered a stinging rebuke of those who feed the public a diet of base and disrespectful programming. This intellectual funnyman offered a final warning. Said Allen: "We have talent and brains. We should be able to bring about laughter and entertainment without sinking into a lack of reverence for decency and sexuality. We're better than that as a people, and the TV industry should reflect the best of our human condition and not the worst." Steve Allen, greatly gifted, humble person, searcher of faith, man who made a difference for the good: I hope he has found all he longed for.

Question for Reflection

● Was Steve Allen's warning about the TV industry too harsh?

Like an Uncle

BISHOP John McGann died in January, 2002. For those of you who did not know this man who led Long Island's Roman Catholic Diocese of Rockville Centre from 1976 until 2000, I'd like to tell you something about him—and the unique relationship between a priest and his bishop.

I first met this wonderful man about 36 years ago, when he attended the graduation of my grammar school classmate, his niece, Kathleen McGann. He was secretary to the bishop then and considered a "comer" in the diocese. When you hear that someone's a noted or popular person, you also expect a certain amount of pretension or self-importance. He had none of that. In fact, he was just what you'd expect of a proud uncle. Over the years I learned that Bishop McGann was always the good uncle you could talk with and enjoy.

I really came to love and respect him when I shared a rectory with him for eight years. He genuinely enjoyed priestly company and fully entered into our communal life. He enjoyed a good drink, a fine meal and lively conversation as well as anyone. And while it's not uncommon for bishops to live in their own residence, he chose to live in a parish rectory. I think he did that out of a true love for priests and parishioners.

As Bishop McGann's coordinator for Family Life, I often asked him to support new initiatives. He was rarely afraid of trying something different, especially if it helped to rescue people from families in trouble. So he endorsed and supported new ventures like Retrouvaille (the program for marriages in crisis), Project Rachel (to heal those who've been through abortion) and the Diocesan Respect Life Council. Bishop McGann also promoted alternatives to abortion like residences for women in crisis pregnancies. As he'd often tell me: "It's not enough to be against abortion unless we also provide life-affirming alternatives. We can't leave the mother and her child with words. We need to give her real support." He was as good as his word.

In 1985 I came to him with a proposal. Would he be willing to be the first bishop of a diocese to peacefully demonstrate outside an abortion facility? As long as it was both peaceful and prayerful, he said he'd be there. That day will be forever etched in the memories of the 4,000 people who heard him speak eloquently about the sanctity of life, then, rosary in hand, prayed us through this important public witness.

Bishop McGann was sometimes accused, falsely, of being weak in support of Catholic education. That wasn't my experience at all. When I became a pastor, I was concerned about the parish school I was inheriting. It happened to be the same school I had attended and I didn't want to be the one to have to close my own alma mater. He told me not to worry, that the school would survive and prosper. His support was unequivocal.

Sometimes, when noted people die, we tend to write of them as if all was perfect. That would be as inaccurate of John McGann as it would of anyone else. Personally, we had a few battles in which we agreed to disagree. But here's the good part: he could disagree with you strongly and still sit down right afterwards for a friendly meal. He knew that people often differ, but it didn't mean he had to like them less. I'm not sure Bishop McGann would be the bishop of a diocese if they were picking one today. He didn't have a ton of academic degrees. He wasn't politically well-connected in the Church. He was just a good, pastoral, hardworking, people-loving, self-aware man struggling to give his all for a Church he loved immensely.

He was always in his heart a parish priest, a favorite uncle, who just happened to occupy the office of bishop.

Question for Reflection

● Why is the virtue of humility often not highly regarded or practiced?

Remembering Bhopal

DOMINIQUE Lapierre fills a room. Not only is he physically striking, but he has an amazing energy and enthusiasm. I first met this charismatic Frenchman after the publication of his book, *The City of Joy*. In it, Lapierre transformed a world of absolute poverty into a place of new life and new hope. He used the setting of Calcutta and the lives of its most disadvantaged people—and those like Mother Teresa, who worked to help them—to show how one individual from the world of the "haves" was transformed by the "have nots." He also explained that poverty can be far more than the absence of material goods; it can also be the lack of community experienced by many who know the privileges of abundance. The Christophers designated *The City of Joy* as a winner of one of our annual book awards for reminding us of the things that really matter.

That volume was one of several that Lapierre has written or co-authored. Because his books have sold millions of copies in over thirty languages, he is a man of means who could simply relax and enjoy his home in Paris. Yet, he finds himself returning often to India.

His latest book, *Five Past Midnight in Bhopal*, is a story of hope. What and where is Bhopal? Sadly, many have probably forgotten. This beautiful city, located in the center of India, is the home of several million people. The American multi-national corporation Union Carbide chose Bhopal as the site of a factory to produce an important pesticide. The intention was good since the chemical had the ability to eradicate many insects that destroy vital Indian crops. At first, the factory was seen as a huge blessing. But on December 3, 1984, at five past midnight, something dreadful happened. A leak in a factory pipeline released deadly gas into the air and winds quickly carried it to the streets and homes of the city. Between 5,000 and 8,000 were estimated to have been killed in the first three days. Many more were blinded or had their lungs destroyed.

Of the approximately half a million people who were affected by the poison gas that night, between 16,000 and 30,000 died from their terrible injuries in the succeeding months and years.

As a widely respected journalist, Dominique Lapierre was invited to assess this tragedy. His study of Bhopal, and the limited and insufficient response of the world community to this industrial calamity profoundly affected him and his wife. They were determined to tell the story of Bhopal to a world that would rather turn away, a world so inundated with painful tales that we sometimes lose a sense of perspective.

Yet, the author believes that many tragedies can be prevented or, at least, alleviated. For example, his years in India alerted him to the dangers of tuberculosis and leprosy. While both conditions are curable, it takes people who care and are able to command the necessary resources to help sick people recover. Dominique Lapierre came to realize that he himself could save lives. So he uses his book royalties to create and sustain clinics that help eradicate TB and leprosy, as well as a new gynecological clinic in Bhopal to treat poor women affected by the disaster. When he is inclined to dismiss his charitable endeavor by seeing it as "just one drop of water" in a vast desert of human need and suffering, he thinks about his friend Mother Teresa, who chided him, "But Dominique, what is the ocean but a collection of many such drops of water?"

Lapierre's visit was really a seminar in Christopher values. He is just one person, but if he hadn't accomplished the good he has, many would be the poorer for it. The same can be said of us. And in joining our caring with the compassion of others, we can be a light that transforms a needful world.

Question for Reflection

● Dominique Lapierre like Blessed Mother Teresa was a strong advocate of the "Power of One." This book is finished. Your job is just beginning. Are you ready to do your part?

Additional Titles Published by Resurrection Press, a Catholic Book Publishing Imprint

A Rachel Rosary *Larry Kupferman*	$4.50
A Season in the South *Marci Alborghetti*	$10.95
Blessings All Around *Dolores Leckey*	$8.95
Catholic Is Wonderful *Mitch Finley*	$4.95
Come, Celebrate Jesus! *Francis X. Gaeta*	$4.95
Days of Intense Emotion *Keeler/Moses*	$12.95
Discernment *Chris Aridas*	$8.95
Feasts of Life *Jim Vlaun*	$12.95
From Holy Hour to Happy Hour *Francis X. Gaeta*	$7.95
Grace Notes *Lorraine Murray*	$9.95
Healing through the Mass *Robert DeGrandis, SSJ*	$9.95
Our Grounds for Hope *Fulton J. Sheen*	$7.95
The Healing Rosary *Mike D.*	$5.95
Healing Your Grief *Ruthann Williams, OP*	$7.95
Heart Peace *Adolfo Quezada*	$9.95
Life, Love and Laughter *Jim Vlaun*	$7.95
The Joy of Being an Altar Server *Joseph Champlin*	$5.95
The Joy of Being a Catechist *Gloria Durka*	$4.95
The Joy of Being a Eucharistic Minister *Mitch Finley*	$5.95
The Joy of Being a Lector *Mitch Finley*	$5.95
The Joy of Being an Usher *Gretchen Hailer, RSHM*	$5.95
The Joy of Marriage Preparation *McDonough/Marinelli*	$5.95
The Joy of Music Ministry *J.M. Talbot*	$6.95
The Joy of Praying the Rosary *James McNamara*	$5.95
The Joy of Preaching *Rod Damico*	$6.95
The Joy of Teaching *Joanmarie Smith*	$5.95
The Joy of Worshiping Together *Rod Damico*	$5.95
Lights in the Darkness *Ave Clark, O.P.*	$8.95
Loving Yourself for God's Sake *Adolfo Quezada*	$5.95
Meditations for Survivors of Suicide *Joni Woelfel*	$8.95
Mother Teresa *Eugene Palumbo, S.D.B.*	$5.95
Mourning Sickness *Keith Smith*	$8.95
Personally Speaking *Jim Lisante*	$8.95
Practicing the Prayer of Presence *Muto/van Kaam*	$8.95
Prayers from a Seasoned Heart *Joanne Decker*	$8.95
Praying the Lord's Prayer with Mary *Muto/vanKaam*	$8.95
5-Minute Miracles *Linda Schubert*	$4.95
Sabbath Moments *Adolfo Quezada*	$6.95
Season of New Beginnings *Mitch Finley*	$4.95
Season of Promises *Mitch Finley*	$4.95
Sometimes I Haven't Got a Prayer *Mary Sherry*	$8.95
St. Katharine Drexel *Daniel McSheffery*	$12.95
Stay with Us *John Mullin, SJ*	$3.95
What He Did for Love *Francis X. Gaeta*	$5.95
Woman Soul *Pat Duffy, OP*	$7.95
You Are My Beloved *Mitch Finley*	$10.95